Published by
EN Productions
P.O. Box 1653, Franklin, TN 37065
www.encountersnetwork.com

Copyright © 2013 James W. Goll
All rights reserved

Unless otherwise indicated, scripture is taken from the
New American Standard Bible®,
Copyright © 1960, 1962, 1963, 1968, 1971, 1972, 1973,
1975, 1977, 1995 by The Lockman Foundation
Used by permission. (www.Lockman.org)

As noted, scripture taken from the HOLY BIBLE, NEW INTERNATIONAL VERSION® (NIV)
Copyright © 1973, 1978, 1984 International Bible Society.
Used by permission of Zondervan. All rights reserved.

Scripture quotations marked (AMP) are taken from the Amplified Bible,
Copyright © 1954, 1958, 1962, 1964, 1965, 1987 by The Lockman Foundation. Used by permission.

As noted, scripture taken from the King James Version (KJV)
The KJV is public domain in the United States.

All scripture is indicated by italics.

GET eSchool and Other Materials

The following *Watchmen on the Walls* study guide is great for individual study in your own home, with a small group, or in a classroom setting. It also serves as part of the core curriculum for a course by the same title in the **God Encounters Training – eSchool of the Heart**, which also includes a corresponding CD or MP3 class set and other related books. Visit www.GETeSchool.com for more information about this and other life-changing courses.

At the end of each detailed lesson are simple questions for your reflection and review. In a back section of this study guide, you will find the answers to these questions to aid in your learning.

If you have benefited from this study guide, James W. Goll has many other study guides and materials available for purchase. You may place orders for materials from Encounters Network's Resource Center on the website at www.encountersnetwork.com or by calling 1-877-200-1604. You may also mail your orders to P.O. Box 470470, Tulsa, OK, 74147-0470. For more information, visit the website or send an e-mail to info@encountersnetwork.com.

Dedication and Acknowledgment

This set of study guides, *Watchmen on the Walls* is dedicated to my dear mother, Amanda Elizabeth Goll. The book of Romans tells us that we are to *"owe no man anything except love"*. Over the years, I watched my mother turn the other cheek many times and sow a prayer of blessing.

On July 3, 1951, my mother told the Lord, *"If you will give me a son, I will dedicate him to Christ's service."* Exactly one year later to the date, on July 3, 1952, I was born. I believe my mother prayed me into the place I am today. Heaven is fuller and earth much emptier but I believe God is still answering the prayers of my dear mom.

I believe that this first study guide, *Watchmen on the Walls,* is still some of my best material on intercession to date. Therefore, it is with great joy that I dedicate the first and the best to the one who impacted my life the most in the place of prayer. Thanks, Lord, for a praying Mom!

With Love and Gratitude,

Dr. James W. Goll

Table of Contents

Preface: Watchmen on the Walls 9

SECTION ONE: THE TASK OF INTERCESSION

Lesson One: Our High Calling to Intercession 15

Lesson Two: Definitions and Examples of an Intercessor 25

Lesson Three: Pleading Our Case 33

Lesson Four: Presenting Our Case 39

Lesson Five: Identification in Intercession 45

Lesson Six: Christ – Our Priestly Model 53

SECTION TWO: RESTORING THE "WATCH OF THE LORD"

Lesson Seven: Fire on the Altar 61

Lesson Eight: Restoring the Ancient Tools 69

Lesson Nine: The Watch of the Lord 77

Lesson Ten: Possessed for Prayer 83

Lesson Eleven: From Prayer to His Presence 89

Lesson Twelve: The House of Prayer for All Nations 95

Answers to the Reflection Questions 103

Resource Materials 105

End Notes 109

Preface: Watchmen on the Walls

Jesus – Our Magnificent Intercessor

As I begin this introductory article for this study guide, *Watchmen on the Walls*, I sense the jealousy of God. Let us exalt Jesus – our Magnificent Intercessor! He, indeed, is altogether lovely. He is the passion of our lives. He is the Father's great mystery and treasure. He is *our Magnificent Intercessor!* Oh, how we have found Him to be *heaven's great prize*!

Let's take a look at three glorious scriptures concerning the intercessory ministry of Jesus. Romans 8:34 tells us, *Christ Jesus is He who died, yes, rather who was raised, who is at the right hand of God, who also intercedes for us.* Hebrews 7:25 unveils to us, *Hence, also He is able to save forever those who draw near to God through Him, since He always lives to make intercession for them.* Lastly, let's look at I John 2:1-2 where it says, *My little children, I am writing these things to you that you may not sin. And if anyone sins, we have an Advocate with the Father, Jesus Christ the righteous; and He Himself is the propitiation for our sins; and not for ours only, but also for those of the whole world.*

The promise of Jesus' priestly-intercessory ministry continuing is undoubtedly found in Scripture. There we are told that His prayer of intercession for believers would be an ongoing expression of His life before God. He *ever* lives to make intercession.

In the Romans 8:34 and Hebrews 7:25 passages, the word "intercede" (*entunchano*) is used. In both cases the word is in the present tense, indicating continuance. It has a range of definitions from "to light upon," "converse with," and "to appeal to."

The English word "intercede" is defined as "to intervene between parties with a view to reconciling differences." In Scripture the word can mean to plead "for" or "against."

Jesus, our magnificent Intercessor, is our most excellent Advocate with the Father. He has stood between us, our sin, and Satan, and by His precious blood made the way open to the Father. He identified with our total depravity and took the sin of all generations past, present and future, and bore it so it could be removed. He has done it all!

Perhaps this glorious Christ could stand before the Father with His arms folded and say something like, "I already did my part. I'm not going to do anything more!" But, *no*! God's tireless Servant ever sits at the Father's right hand to make intercession for a lost generation.

Hebrews 12:24 tells us that there is, before God's throne, *a blood that speaks better than the blood of Abel*. This blood is the precious blood of Jesus. If Abel's blood spoke out from the ground for vengeance, then what does the blood of Jesus cry out? His sacrificial blood continuously cries loudly, **"Mercy!"** Oh, the saving cry of **mercy**!

THE PRAYERS OF JESUS

What is Jesus praying about? John 17:1-26, perhaps, gives us a few insights. In the last section of His prayer (vs. 20-26), Jesus continues His requests to the Father.

Let's look at three requests that the Son of God lifts up.

The first request, in verse 11, is that *...all of them may be one...* This is followed by a statement of mutual affection between the Father and the Son, and that the believers *may also be in us so that the world may believe that you have sent me.*

The second request of Jesus' high priestly prayer, found in verse 21, is also concerned with unity, *that. . .they may be brought to complete unity to let the world know that you sent me. . .*

The last request is found in verse 24, where it states, *"Father, I desire that they also, whom Thou hast given Me, be with Me where I am, in order that they may behold My glory, which Thou hast given Me; for Thou didst love Me before the foundation of the world."* Jesus wants His disciples to be with Him in the presence of the Father. What a tender, intimate prayer. Jesus desires the companionship of all believers for all eternity. What a passionate Lord we have!

JESUS – OUR LIFE AND SOURCE OF PRAYER

Indeed, Jesus is our life. He has shown us the Father. Now we, as New Testament priestly burden-bearers, have the opportunity to go up into the gap on behalf of others. Now, through His life, we can have His Spirit pray His prayers through us to our Father. After all, He lives in us doesn't He? Let us die to self and let Christ live and pray through us, His beloved friends. **Does He deserve any less?**

As you do these twelve lessons in this study guide, may the Father reveal to you the high privilege we each have in being burden bearers for the Lord. Intercession is not actually a hard task. It is a divine opportunity to be a history maker. May the Holy Spirit inspire and equip you to be a co-laborer with Christ. For more on this subject, read my book *The Lost Art of Intercession.*

Blessings to you!

James W. Goll

Section One:

The Task of Intercession

Lesson One:
Our High Calling to Intercession

I. **OUR HIGH CALLING TO INTERCESSION**

   A. **Gary Bergel – Director of Intercessors For America**
   "Our participation in Christ's high priestly ministry of intercession is literally our inheritance, but it is also a rare and precious privilege. For those who have ears to hear, the Spirit of God is issuing an awesome, privileged invitation to the Church in this hour." 'Come! Enter the throne room. Come! Take the royal scepter; conquer and rule with Me! Come! Enjoy friendship with Me. Come ...sit on the throne with Me' (Rev. 2:26-27; 3:21).

   We are being invited close to the heart of God, and He is offering grace to enable us to respond. Effective prayer and intercession is a mark of submission to, friendship with, and fruitful union with the living God."[1]

   B. **M. Basilea Schlink – Author, Teacher, Prayer Leader**
   "The Lord is searching for people who are willing to step into the breach and become bridges for others so that they can turn back to God. God has placed "dynamite" in our hands – the opportunity to step into the breach for others – by our prayers! True, earnest prayer contains the power to transform and release people.

   Earnest prayer makes the intercessor like a king; investing him with authority so great that it can release captives! We must therefore persist in intercession, using the victorious Name of Jesus and the quickened Word of God, until Satan gives up his booty.

   Our willingness to engage in prevailing, earnest prayer will decide the eternal destiny of our neighbor and ourselves! Whoever is not released from Satan's grip in this lifetime will come under Satan's dominion for eternity. They will forever dwell in the realm of horror and terror. Prevailing intercession holds the great promise and responsibility for their release."[2]

   C. **Watchman Nee – Chinese Leader Imprisoned for His Faith**
   "How is God's will to be done on earth? Only by ... remembering ... that the Church at prayer is heaven's outlet, the channel of release for heaven's power, and that this ministry is our greatest possible work."[3]

D. Martin Luther – German Reformer in the 1600's
"We must achieve everything through prayer – to be able to keep what we have and to defend it against our enemies, the devil, and the world. Therefore, it is the particular work of Christians, who have the Spirit of God, to be incessant and constant in their praying."[4]

E. Andrew Murray – Dutch Reformer, Teacher, Author
"God's intense longing to bless seems, in some sense, to be graciously limited by His dependence on intercession. God regards intercession as the highest expression of His people's readiness to receive and to yield themselves wholly to the working of His almighty power. God rules the world and His Church through the prayers of His people. That God should have made the extension of His Kingdom, to such a large extent, dependent on the faithfulness of His people and prayer is a stupendous mystery and yet an absolute certainty."[5]

F. Paul E. Billheimer – Author, *Destined for the Throne*
"That God will do nothing in the realm of human redemption, since its inception, outside of this scheme of prayer and intercession is indicated by God's many pressing invitations to prayer in His Word. He not only invites: He entreats, He importunes, He urges. He even begs us to exercise this privilege. One translator has paraphrased Mt. 7:7 thus: *'Ask, I ask you to ask; seek, I entreat you to seek; knock, I urge you to knock.'* Evidently He can do nothing without our prayers. He not only invites and exhorts us to pray, He also commands!"[6]

G. E. M. Bounds – Writer, Man of Prayer
"God shapes the world by prayer. The more praying there is in the world, the better the world will be and the mightier the forces against evil. God continues His cause and purpose of life on earth through the eternal value of prayer."[7]

H. John Wesley – Revivalist Preacher
"God will do nothing but in answer to prayer."[8]

I. S. D. Gordon – Noted Prayer Leader
"The greatest thing anyone can do for God and for man is to pray. You can do more than pray after you've prayed. But you cannot do more than pray – until you've prayed."[9]

J. Larry Lea – Prayer Leader, Author
"Prayer is not meant to be drudgery or mere ritual. Neither is prayer a way to "twist the arm" of God so He will do something He does not really want to do. Rather, prayer is coming into agreement with what God has already done in Jesus Christ and getting to the place where our petitions harmonize with what Jesus Himself is praying.

Jesus is calling His Church to intercede. Realizing that the desire to pray is not something we can work up in our flesh, why not pause right now and ask the Holy Spirit to plant or renew the desire in your heart to pray, and that He be your guide into a new discipline and delight in prayer."[10]

II. A KINGDOM OF PRIESTS

A. A Royal Priesthood

1. I Pet. 2:9 – *You are a chosen race, a royal priesthood, a holy nation, a people for God's own possession, that you may proclaim the excellencies of Him who has called you out of darkness into His marvelous light.*

2. Rev. 1:6 – *He has made us to be a kingdom, priests to His God and Father; to Him be the glory and the dominion forever and ever. Amen.*

3. Rev. 5:10 – *And Thou hast made them to be a kingdom and priests to our God, and they will reign upon the earth.*

4. Rom. 5:17 – *For if by the transgression of the one, death reigned through the one, much more those who receive the abundance of grace and of the gift of righteousness will reign in life through the One, Jesus Christ.*

5. I Pet. 2:5 – *You also, as living stones, are being built up as a spiritual house for a holy priesthood, to offer up spiritual sacrifices acceptable to God through Jesus Christ.*

B. Continual Sacrifices

1. Ex. 30:1,7-9 – *You shall make an altar as a place for burning incense …and Aaron shall burn fragrant incense on it …every morning when he trims the lamps. And when Aaron trims the lamps at twilight, he shall burn incense. There shall be perpetual incense before the Lord throughout your generations.*

2. Lev. 6:9, 12-13 – *Command Aaron and his sons, saying, 'This is the law for the burnt offering: the burnt offering itself shall remain on the hearth on the altar all night until the morning, and the fire on the altar is to be kept burning on it …and the fire on the altar shall be kept burning on it. It shall not go out, but the priest shall burn wood on it every morning; and he shall lay out the burnt*

offering on it, and offer up in smoke the fat portions of the peace offering on it. Fire shall be kept burning continually on the altar; it is not to go out.

3. Lev. 24:2-3 – *Command the sons of Israel that they bring to you clear oil from beaten olives for the light, to make a lamp burn continually. Outside the veil of testimony in the tent of meeting, Aaron shall keep it in order from evening to morning before the Lord continually; it shall be a perpetual statute throughout your generations.*

C. Spiritual Sacrifices

1. Heb. 13:15 – *...let us continually offer up a sacrifice of praise to God, that is, the fruit of lips that give thanks to His name.*

2. Ps. 100 – *Shout joyfully to the Lord, all the earth. Serve the Lord with gladness; come before Him with joyful singing... enter His gates with thanksgiving, and His courts with praise. Give thanks to Him; bless His name. For the Lord is good; His loving kindness is everlasting, and His faithfulness to all generations.*

3. Rev. 5:1-3, 7-10 – *And I saw in the right hand of Him that sat on the throne a book written within and on the backside, sealed with seven seals. And I saw a strong angel proclaiming with a loud voice, who is worthy to open the book, and to loose the seals thereof? And no man in heaven, nor in earth, neither under the earth, was able to open the book, neither to look thereon ...and He came and took the book out of the right hand of Him that sat upon the throne. And when He had taken the book, the four beasts and four and twenty elders fell down before the Lamb, having every one of them harps, and golden vials full of odors, which are the prayers of saints. And they sung a new song, saying, Thou art worthy to take the book, and to open the seals thereof: for thou was slain, and hast redeemed us to God by thy blood out of every kindred, and tongue, and people, and nation; And hast made us unto our God kings and priests: and we shall reign on the earth.*

4. Rev. 8:3-5 – *And another angel came and stood at the altar, holding a golden censer; and much incense was given to him, that he might add it to the prayers of all the saints upon the golden altar which was before the throne. And the smoke of the incense, with the prayers of the saints, went up before God out of the angel's hand...*

5. From Ed Sandquist – Pastor, Psalmist from New York
"Another look at the passage in Revelation 5 sheds some additional light on this for those who would be effective intercessors. Here we see Jesus, the Lion of Judah, the Son of David, the Lamb of God, seated upon the throne of God. He holds the scroll of man's destiny in His powerful grasp. Remember, no one else has the scroll or can even look into it. God sealed it and Jesus is the only one authorized to open the seals and bring God's purposes to pass concerning man and all of creation. He, then, is the only one before whom it could possibly do any good to intercede. Glorious worship is the context of the saints' prayer offering. This worship is part of the homage, which is due the King. It is celebration, rejoicing, and thanks-giving for the earthly rule of the Lamb/Lion/God/Man who reigns."11

6. Derek Prince – International Teacher
"In Numbers 16:46-48, Aaron provides a vivid picture of the intercessor. The congregation of Israel had sinned by rebellion against their leaders and God sent judgment upon them in the form of a plague that was taking the lives of thousands.

Moses told Aaron (the high priest), *'Take a censer, and put fire therein from the altar, and put on incense, and go quickly into the congregation, and make an atonement for them for there is wrath gone out from the Lord, the plague is begun.'*

Aaron put the incense into his censer and ran out into the midst of the congregation. There, he took his stand between those who had already been smitten by the plague and those who had not. The fragrant smoke, ascending from the censer as Aaron swung it to and fro, formed a line to divide between two groups. *'He stood between the dead and the living; and the plague was stayed.'*

The smoke of the incense from Aaron's censer typifies *'the effectual prayer of a righteous man'* (Jas. 5:16). **Where intercession took effect, the plague ceased. Judgment ended and mercy began."**12

III. INTERCESSION DEFINED

A. *Webster's* Dictionary Definitions

1. Intercede – (Latin *intercedo*: *inter* – between; *ado* – to go; literally, to pass between) to act between parties with a view to reconcile those who differ or contend; to plead in favor of another; to interpose, to mediate or make intercession.
2. Mediate – being between two extremes; to interpose between parties at variance with a view to reconciliation; to mediate a peace.
3. Mediation – "entreaty for another – intercession."

B. Hebrew Definition:[13]

The Hebrew word for intercession is *'paga'*, which is only translated a few times as intercession in the Old Testament. Yet, when you compare the many different pictures, words, and interpretations of the word *paga*, you can glean many wonderful understandings of what it means to intercede. *Paga* – to meet, to light upon (by chance), to fall upon, attack, strike down, cut down, to strike the mark, laid upon.

1. To meet – Is. 64:5. A meeting with God for the purpose of reconciliation.
2. To light upon – Gen. 28:10-17. By God's working of grace, our divine "Helper" is standing by, ready to aid us in our intercession, moving us from the natural to the supernatural, from finite ability to infinite ability, taking hold of situations with us so as to accomplish the will of God.
3. To fall upon, attack, strike down, cut down – I Sam. 22:11-19; II Sam. 1:11-16. Intercession is the readiness of a soldier to fall upon or attack the enemy at the command of his lord, striking and cutting him down!
4. To strike the mark – Job 36:32. Intercession releases the flashing forth of His glory/lightening, directing it to the desired situation and allowing it to strike the mark.
5. Laid upon – Is. 53:12 (intercession); Is. 53:6 (laid upon). Intercession reached its fullest and most profound expression when our sins were "laid upon" Jesus. Jesus was able to fully identify with us, having the totality of our condition placed upon Himself; then as the scapegoat, He carried it far away. There is an aspect of this form of intercession into which we, as His Body, can enter. Col. 1:24 calls us to *share on behalf of His body, which is the Church, in filling up that which is lacking in Christ's afflictions.*

C. Closing Prayer

May the Lord's eyes pass our way and light upon us. May the spirit of prayer come upon us and grip us in this generation for these purposes in Jesus mighty Name! Amen!

Reflection Questions
Lesson One: Our High Calling to Intercession

Answers to these questions can be found in the back of the study guide.

Fill in the Blank

1. What is one of our inheritances in Christ? _____

2. God rules the world and His church through the _____ of His people.

3. God will do _____ but in answer to prayer.

Multiple Choice – Choose the best answer from the list below:

A.	spiritual	C.	sacrifice
B.	thanksgiving	D.	intercession

4. You also, as living stones are being built up as a _____ house for a holy priesthood.

5. Let us continually offer up a _____ of praise to God.

True or False

6. The fragrant smoke from Aaron's censor stopped the plague upon Israel. _____

7. The Lord is searching for people who are willing to pray. _____

8. Basilea Schlink said, "Our willingness to engage in prevailing, earnest prayer will decide the eternal destiny of our neighbor and ourselves. _____

Continued on the next page.

Scripture Memorization

9. Write out I Peter 2:9 and memorize it.

10. What was the primary insight you gained from this lesson, and how will you apply it to your life?

Lesson Two:
Definitions and Examples of an Intercessor

I. **FOUR DISTINCT BIBLICAL DEFINITIONS OF AN INTERCESSOR**

   A. **An intercessor is one who reminds the Lord of promises and appointments yet to be met and fulfilled.**
   Isaiah 62:6-7 – *On your walls, O Jerusalem, I have appointed watchmen; all day and all night they will never keep silent. You who remind the Lord, take no rest for yourselves; and give Him no rest until He establishes and makes Jerusalem a praise in the earth.*

   B. **An intercessor is one who takes up a case of justice before God on behalf of another.**
   Isaiah 59:15-16 – *Yes truth is lacking; and he turns aside from evil and makes himself a prey. Now the Lord saw, and it was displeasing in His sight that there was no justice. And He saw that there was no man, and was astonished* (appalled) *that there was no one to intercede.*

   C. **An intercessor is one who makes up the hedge; builds up the wall in a time of battle.**
   Ezekiel 13:4-5 – *O Israel, your prophets have been like foxes among ruins. You have not gone up into the breaches* (breaks), *nor did you build the wall* (hedge) *around the house of Israel to stand in the battle on the day of the Lord.*

   D. **An intercessor is one who stands in the gap between God's righteous judgments that are due and the need for mercy on the people's behalf.**
   Ezekiel 22:30-31 – *And I searched for a man among them who should build up the wall and stand in the gap before Me for the land, that I should not destroy it; but I found no one. Thus I have poured out my indignation on them; I have consumed them with the fire of My wrath; their way I have brought upon their heads, declares the Lord God.*

II. **HISTORICAL AND BIBLICAL EXAMPLES**

   A. **Praying Hyde – Pioneer of Prayer in Northern India**
   Think of Praying Hyde. He often went into the hills to visit friends and pray. A friend relates, "It was evident to all he was bowed down with sore travail of soul. He missed many meals and when I went to his room, I would find him lying as in great agony, or walking up and down as if an inward fire were burning in his bones." It was from intense burden that Hyde asked God to give him **a soul a day that**

year. Praying Hyde departed from his friends no ordinary man. He became a burden-bearer for mankind. At year's end, **four hundred souls had been won to Christ!** As the New Year came, John Hyde approached God's throne with a greater burden. Now Hyde begged for **two souls daily**. Twelve months later, more had been won than Hyde anticipated. In fact, some **eight hundred souls** were claimed that year. This, however, did not satisfy Praying Hyde. Soon we hear him pleading, **"Give me four souls every day."**

Hyde's intent was not to win these with tent crusades or massive rallies. He went for every soul, one at a time. It is said that Hyde approached sinners on the street of any village at any time. Conversation ensued and before long, both would kneel in prayer. Hyde would lead this new convert to water and perform baptismal rites. This event repeated itself four times daily because Hyde's burden reached out to lost men. Multitudes of souls found Christ when this humble man assumed a burden for the lost.[14]

B. **Father Nash – Intercessor for Revivalist Charles Finney**
    Through past centuries, revivals of consequence have come through intercessory prayer. Finney's revival rocked America's Eastern states in the **first half of the nineteenth century**. One man, known as **Father Nash, would precede Finney to cities scheduled for crusades.** Three or four weeks in advance of meetings, Father Nash humbly journeyed to town. No great crowds waited to welcome him and no bands played fanfares of greeting. Father Nash would quietly find a place of prayer. During the revivals, countless souls were won and lives changed. Finney's name soon gained acclaim and his sermons pierced the hearts of multitudes.

    Somewhere alone, however, knelt humble Father Nash. After revival came, he quietly left town for another crusade, there to labor on bended knees. He, too, knew the meaning of intercession. Father Nash concerned himself with others, often sacrificing the finer things of life.

    He had no home, no church support, and often missed the taste of home-cooked meals. Nights were spent without a bed, and clothes became frayed.

    What did Nash receive for this?
    Little in this life, perhaps, but much in the life to come. He owns stock in two and one-half million Finney converts. Few realize how many souls found Christ because of Father Nash. **Time, no doubt, will show that behind every soul won for Christ was intercessory prayer.** Indeed, Finney had remarkable talent to preach. Certainly

he had a special touch from God. **But mark this fact – every Finney needs a Father Nash! Every preacher needs an intercessor.**[15]

C. Ephesians 6:18
With all prayer and petition, pray at all times in the Spirit and with this view in mind, be on the alert with all perseverance and petition for all the saints.

D. I Peter 4:7
The end of all things is at hand, therefore be of sound judgment and sober spirit for the purpose of prayer.

E. Isaiah 63:15-19; 64:1, 2, 4, 7
Look down from heaven, and see from Thy holy and glorious habitation. Where are Thy zeal and Thy mighty deeds? The stirrings of Thy heart and Thy compassion are restrained toward me, For Thou art our Father, though Abraham does not know us, And Israel does not recognize us. Thou, O Lord, art our Father, Our Redeemer from of old is Thy name. Why, O Lord, dost Thou cause us to stray from Thy ways, And harden our heart from fearing Thee? Return for the sake of Thy servants, the tribes of Thy heritage. Thy holy people possessed Thy sanctuary for a little while, our adversaries have trodden it down. We have become like those over whom Thou hast never ruled, like those who were not called by Thy name.

Oh, that Thou wouldst rend the heavens and come down, that the mountains might quake at Thy presence as fire kindles the brushwood, as fire causes water to boil to make Thy name known to Thine adversaries, that the nations may tremble at Thy presence ...for from of old thy have not heard nor perceived by ear, neither has the eye seen a God besides Thee, who acts in behalf of the one who waits for Him ...and there is no one who calls on Thy name, who arouses himself to take hold of Thee; for Thou hast hidden Thy face from us, and hast delivered us into the power of our iniquities.

F. Hebrews 7:25
Hence He is able to save forever those who draw near to God through Him, since He always lives to make intercession for them (the historic example and ongoing ministry of our Savior Jesus Christ).

G. Prophetic Statement
The Prophetic word which came to Dick Simmons – Prayer Leader of Men for the Nations – "If they don't pray, all that I can do is watch them try to do what I want to do for them."

III. THE INVITATION EXTENDED

A. Ezekiel 36:37
Thus says the Lord God, "This also I will let the House of Israel ask Me to do for them; I will increase their men like a flock."

God is saying, "**I WILL LET YOU ASK ME TO DO WHAT I WANT TO DO FOR YOU!**"

This is our invitation and high privilege to change history by untying God's hands through prayer!

B. The Passionate Cry from Andrew Murray
"Disciples of Jesus! You are called to be like your Lord in His priestly intercession! When will we awaken to the glory of our destiny to pray to God for perishing men and be answered? When will we shake off the sloth that clothes itself in the pretense of humility and yield ourselves wholly to God's Spirit, that He might fill our wills with light and power to know, to take, and to possess everything that our God is waiting to give?"

Lord, teach us to pray.

"O my Blessed High Priest! Who am I that You should invite me to share Your power of intercession? And why, O my Lord, am I so slow of heart to understand, believe, and exercise this wonderful privilege to which You have redeemed Your people?

O Lord! Give me Your grace, that my life's work may become praying without ceasing, to draw down the blessing of heaven on all my surroundings on earth.

Blessed Lord! I come now to accept my calling, for which I will give up everything and follow You. Into Your hands I will willingly yield my whole being. Form, train, and inspire me to be one of Your prayer force, those who watch and strive in prayer, who have power and victory. Take possession of my heart, and fill it with the desire to glorify God in the gathering, sanctification, and union of those whom the Father has given You. Take my mind and give me wisdom to know when prayer can bring a blessing. Take me wholly and prepare me as You would a priest, to stand always before God and to bless His Name.

Blessed Lord! Now and through all my spiritual life, let me want everything for You, and nothing for myself. Let it be my experience that the person who has and asks for nothing for himself, receives everything, including the wonderful grace of sharing Your everlasting ministry of intercession. Amen."[16]

Reflection Questions
Lesson Two: Definitions and Examples of an Intercessor

Answers to these questions can be found in the back of the study guide.

Fill in the Blank

1. An Intercessor is one who takes up a case of _____ before God on behalf of another.

2. An Intercessor is one who makes up the _____; builds up the wall.

3. *"Lord teach us to _____"* was the request of the disciples to Jesus.

Multiple Choice – Choose the best answer from the list below:

      A. indignation   C. reminds
      B. gap   D. petition

4. An Intercessor is one who _____ the Lord of promises.

5. *And I searched for a man among them who should build up the wall and stand in the _____.*

True or False

6. Praying Hyde ask God for two souls a day and God answered his prayer. _____

7. We are not to press God for an answer, just ask once and wait for the answer. _____

8. Time will show that behind every soul won for Christ was intercessory prayer. _____

Continued on the next page.

Scripture Memorization

9. Write out Ephesians 6:18 and memorize it.

10. What was the primary insight you gained from this lesson, and how will you apply it to your life?

Lesson Three:
Pleading Our Case

A Biblical Basis for Pleading Our Argumentation before God

I. **BIBLICAL PRECEDENT TO PLEAD**

   A. **Definitions of "Plead"**

   1. *Webster's Dictionary* – to argue a case in a court of law; to entreat or appeal earnestly.

   2. Hebrew – (*shâphat*) to judge, pronounce sentence, vindicate, punish, or to litigate.

   B. **God as Judge**
   We must have a revelation that God is the Judge and we have a rightful position to present our case through our Advocate/Lawyer – Jesus Christ, the Righteous!

   1. Heb. 12:22-24.
      a) First, we find a description of God's dwelling place.
      b) Second, those who dwell there with God.
      c) Third, the presentation of God Himself.
         (1) God as Judge of all.
         (2) Jesus as the Mediator.
         (3) Blood, which "speaks."

   2. Gen. 18:25 – Abraham's plea to the Lord, *Shall not the Judge of all the earth do right?*

   3. Judg. 11:27 – *The Lord be the Judge this day.*

   4. Is. 33:22 – *For the Lord is our Judge.*

   C. **Prevailing upon the Unrighteous Judge**
   Luke 18:1-8 (especially vs. 6-7) – *And the Lord said, "Hear what the unrighteous judge said! Now shall not God bring about justice for His elect, who cry out to Him day and night, and will He delay long over them? I tell you that He will bring about justice for them speedily."*

D. **Primary Verse – Isaiah 43:26**

1. KJV – *Put Me in remembrance; let us **plead** together: declare thou, that thou mayest be justified.*
2. NASB – *Put Me in remembrance; let us **argue** our case together; state your cause that you may be proved right.*
3. TLB – *Oh, remind Me of this promise of forgiveness, for we must talk about your sins. **Plead** your case for My forgiving you.*

Presenting your case and detailing your arguments not only pleases God, it also helps you understand your need more completely, moves your compassion, strengthens your determination, and arms you with greater holy hunger.

II. EXAMPLES OF PLEADING

A. **Isaiah 1:18**
Come, now, let us reason together says the Lord. This is an invitation to a court-type hearing; a court of appeal at the throne of God.

B. **Job 23:3-5**
If only I knew where to find Him, if only I could go to His dwelling! I would state my case before Him and fill my mouth with arguments. I would find out what He would answer me. Moffott translates Job as saying, 'Oh that I knew... how to reach His very throne, and there lay my case before Him, arguing it out in full.'

C. **Quote of Charles Spurgeon – English Pulpiteer**
"It is the habit of faith, when she is praying, to use pleas. Mere prayer sayers, who do not pray at all, forget to argue with God; but those who would prevail bring forth their reasons and their strong arguments [...] faith's act of wrestling is to plead with God and say with holy boldness, 'Let it be thus and thus, for these reasons.' He preached, the man who has his mouth full of arguments in prayer shall soon have his mouth full of benedictions in answer to prayer."[17]

D. **Quote of Wesley Duewel – Author, Missionary Statesman**
"This holy argumentation with God is not done in a negative, complaining spirit. It is the expression not of a critical heart but of a heart burning with love for God, for His Name, and for His glory. This holy debate with God is a passionate presentation to God of the many reasons why it will be in harmony with His nature, His righteous government, and the history of His holy intervention on behalf of His people."

"You do not plead like a negative, legal adversary in the presence of God the holy Judge. Rather, you plead in the form of a well-prepared brief, prepared by a legal advocate on behalf of a need and for the welfare of the Kingdom. At times you are, as it were, petitioning God's court for an injunction against Satan to stop his harassment. The Holy Spirit guides you in the preparation and wording of your prayer argument."[18]

E. Jeremiah 14:7, 21
O Lord, do something for the sake of Thy name. Do not dishonor Your glorious throne.

F. Joshua 7:9
Joshua pleaded with God to help Israel, asking, *What Thou will do for Your own name sake?*

G. Joel 2:17
Let the priests, the Lord's ministers, weep between the porch and the altar and let them say, 'Spare Thy people, Oh Lord. And do not make Thine inheritance a reproach, a byword amongst the nations.' Why should they among the peoples say, 'Where is their God?'

H. Genesis 18:22-33

1. Abraham pleaded and humbly argued the justice of God. How could God punish the righteous with the wicked (v. 23)?

2. He pleaded for the wicked to be spared for the sake of the righteous, and he pleaded again for God's justice for the righteous (v. 24).

3. Abraham argued from the righteous character of God (v.25).

4. Repeatedly Abraham pleaded, "Don't be angry with me, but let me plead one more time." Did God become angry? Absolutely not. He loved and honored Abraham all the more for his longing for God's righteous mercy, for longing for the doomed sinners. Abraham had a heart like God's. God always longs to be merciful. Abraham proved himself the friend of God (Jas. 2:23) by his holy pleading and bargaining for mercy.

I. Closing Thoughts
Can we do the same? The Lord is looking in this generation for those who will stand in the gap and make a difference in their generation. Volunteer now to answer His call for intercessors to come forth!

Reflection Questions
Lesson Three: Pleading Our Case

Answers to these questions can be found in the back of the study guide.

Fill in the Blank

1. *Come, now, let us _____ together says the _____.*

2. Joshua _____ with God to help Israel.

3. It is the habit of faith, when she is praying to use _____.

Multiple Choice – Choose the best answer from the list below:

      A.   judge   C.   presence

      B.   revelation   D.   inhabitants

4. The Lord be the _____ this day.

5. We must have a _____ that God is the Judge.

True or False

6. The holy argumentation with God is done with a complaining spirit. _____

7. Abraham pleaded and humbly argued the justice of God. _____

8. Abraham argued for the righteous character of God. _____

Continued on the next page.

Scripture Memorization

9. Write out Psalm. 19:14 and memorize it.

10. What was the primary insight you gained from this lesson, and how will you apply it to your life?

Lesson Four: Presenting Our Case

A Biblical Basis for Presenting Our Argumentation before God

I. **KNOW THE PROMISE**
   Research, know, and remind God of His promises.

   A. **Written, Unfulfilled Bible Promises**
      Is. 62:6-7 – *I have set watchmen upon thy walls, O Jerusalem, which shall never hold their peace day nor night: ye that make mention of the Lord, keep not silence. And give Him no rest, till He establishes, and till He makes Jerusalem a praise in the earth.*

   B. **Present Day, Unfulfilled Yet True, Prophetic Promises**
      I Tim. 1:18-19 – *This charge I commit unto thee, son Timothy, according to the prophecies which went before on thee, that thou by them mightest war a good warfare; Holding faith, and a good conscience; which some having put away concerning faith have made shipwreck;*

II. **PRESENT THE ARGUMENT**

   A. **Speaking the Promises Back to God**
      We require the Lord to watch over His Word and perform it (Jer. 1:12). We now remind Him of His promises with holy boldness that have not yet been met and fulfilled.

   B. **Purity of Motive – A Necessity!**
      Be sure our own heart is pure before God and that there is no controversy between God and our own soul. Be sure to argue for that which is in accordance with God's will, which extends God's Kingdom, and which glorifies God.

III. **SEVEN BASIS OF APPEAL** [19]

   A. **Plead the Honor and Glory of God's Name**

      1. God saved Israel at the Red Sea *for His name's sake* (Ps. 106:8).
      2. Samuel prayed for the sake of God's own Name (II Sam. 7:26).

3. David, knowing the God-given responsibility of kingship placed upon him, prayed for guidance (Ps. 23:3; 31:3) and help (Ps. 109:21; 143:11) and for God's Name's sake.
4. Asaph prayed for God to help Israel *"for the glory of Your holy name"* (Ps. 79:9).

B. Plead God's Relationships to Us

1. God is our **Creator** and we are the work of His hands (Job 10:3, 8, 9; 14:15; Ps. 119:73).
2. God is our **Helper** (Ps. 33:20; 40:17; 63:7); our ever-present help (Ps. 46:1).
3. God is our **Redeemer** (Ps. 19:14; Is. 41:14; 54:5); He will have compassion on us because He is our Redeemer (Is. 54:8; 63:16).
4. God is our **Father** (Is. 64:8; Mal. 3:17; Rom. 8:15); cry as a child to His Father, "Abba!"
5. As our Creator, Helper, Redeemer, and Father, we plead for His protection and provision for all He has created and redeemed!

C. Plead God's Attributes

1. Plead God's **righteousness** as Nehemiah did (Neh. 9:33). Christ speeds the cause of the righteous (Is. 16:5).
2. Plead on the basis of God's **faithfulness.** In Psalm 89, Ethan makes God's faithfulness the basis of his plea **six times**!
3. Plead on the basis of God's **mercy** and **love**. Join Moses (Dcut. 9:18), David (Ps. 4:1; 27:7; 30:10; 86:6, 15-16), Daniel and the three Hebrew children (Dan. 2:18).
4. Spurgeon stated, "We shall find every attribute of God Most High to be, as it were, a great battering ram with which we may open the gates of heaven."

D. Plead the Sorrows and Needs of the People

1. David was one who took on himself the sufferings of his people. He even wept for the suffering of his enemies (Ps. 16:9). Nehemiah, and especially Daniel, also used this plea greatly as they vicariously identified themselves with the sufferings of the people.
2. Jeremiah, perhaps more powerfully than others, used this form of plea as he prevailed for his people. He pleads for God to look and see the sufferings (Lam. 2:20), to remember, look, and see (5:1). In great detail he lists for God all the sufferings of the people. He does not try to justify his people, for he knows how deserving they are of God's judgments. Yet he pleads on the basis of their sufferings.

E. Plead the Past Answers to Prayer

1. David reminded God of His past mercy: *"You have been my helper* (Ps. 27:9). *Since my youth, O God, you have taught me [...] Even when I am old and gray, do not forsake me, O God"* (Ps. 71:17-18). A number of the Psalms remind God and the people in detail of His past mercies (78; 85:1-7; 105-106; 136).
2. Present pleading arguments for new mercies on the basis of the history of all He has already done. But the task is unfinished. God has invested too much to stop now. Plead for God's mercy and power to be renewed to bring final victory.

F. Plead the Word and the Promises of God

1. David held God to His word. Reverently, humbly, lovingly, but with holy insistence, David pressed for the fulfillment of God's promise. *"Do as You promised [...] that Your name will be great forever [...] So your servant has found courage to pray to you. O Lord, You are God! You have promised these good things to Your servant"* (I Chron.17:23-26).
2. Solomon prayed the same way. He held God to the promises He had made to David, his father. *"O Lord, God of Israel, there is no God like You in heaven or on earth – You who keep Your covenant of love [...] You have kept your promise to your servant David my father [...] Now Lord [...] keep for Your servant David, my father, the promises You made to him when You said [...] And now, O Lord, God of Israel, let Your word that You promised Your servant David come true"* (II Chron. 6:14-17). This was no mincing of words. God had spoken. Now Solomon insisted that God fulfill His word.

G. Plead the Blood of Jesus

1. Perhaps the greatest, most powerful, most unanswerable plea of all is the blood of Jesus. There is not a more prevailing argument that we can bring before God than the sufferings, blood, and death of His Son. We have no merit of our own. We do not prevail by prayer techniques or past experience. There is no prayer "know-how" that overcomes. It is only through the blood of Jesus.

2. Bring before the Father the wounds of Jesus; remind the Father of the agony in Gethsemane; recall to the Father the strong cries of the Son of God as He prevailed for our world and for our salvation. Remind the Father of Earth's darkest hour on Calvary, as the Son triumphed alone for you and me. Shout to heaven again Christ's triumphant call, *It is finished!* Plead the cross. Plead the blood. Plead them over and over again.
3. Plead the blood. Pray until you have the assurance of God's will. Pray until you have been given by the Spirit a vision of what God longs to do, needs to do, and waits to do. Pray until the authority of the Name of Jesus grips you. Then plead the blood of Jesus. The Name of Jesus and the blood of Jesus – glory in them, stake your all on them, and use them to the glory of God and the routing of Satan.
4. Spurgeon said, "This is that which unlocks the treasury of heaven. Many keys fit many locks, but the master key is the blood and the Name of Him that died and rose again, and ever lives in heaven to save unto the uttermost."

IV. THE RESULT

Isaiah 43:26 – *Put me in remembrance, let us argue our case together. State your cause,* ***that you may be proved right.***

Isn't it amazing? God calls us into an "interactive relationship" with Him through prayer. He wants us to "pin Him down" and win! He invites us into a courtroom hearing and He wants us to win.

Reflection Questions
Lesson Four: Presenting Our Case

Answers to these questions can be found in the back of the study guide.

Fill in the Blank

1. Research, _____ and remind God of His promises.

2. We speak the _____ back to God and remind Him of His Word.

3. God is our _____ and we are the work of His hands.

Multiple Choice – Choose the best answer from the list below:

      A.   faithfulness   C.   righteousness

      B.   Redeemer   D.   sufferings

4. God is our _____.

5. David was one who took on himself the _____ of his people.

True or False

6. A few of God's attributes are righteousness, faithfulness, love and mercy. _____

7. Pray until you have the assurance of God's will. _____

8. God wants us to "pin Him down" and win. _____

Continued on the next page.

Scripture Memorization

9. Write out Isaiah 43:26 and memorize it.

10. What was the primary insight you gained from this lesson, and how will you apply it to your life?

Lesson Five:
Identification in Intercession

I. WHAT IS "IDENTIFICATION" ANYWAY?

A. A Lost Art

This is perhaps one of the highest and most overlooked aspects of true intercession. It is identifying with the needs of the people to such an extent that in your heart you seem to "become one with them." Out of a heart of compassion, contrition, and desperation, your heart pounds with the sufferings of others as though it were your own. As you receive the heart of the Father, by the spirit of revelation, **it is your own**. You identify with God's righteous judgments, His desire for mercy, the peoples' horrifying condition, and their sins, which block the way. Then, by **choosing** to be **"one of them,"** and laying aside your own position, your heart is burdened by the Spirit of God and a cry of confession of sin, disgrace, failure, and humiliation quietly and sometimes dramatically pours forth from your heart unto the Lord. You carry away the blockage of sin, so as to open the way that God's promises might continue forth.

But this form of intercession is a lost art in the modern day, materialistic, success-oriented society. Let us pray to the Lord for this kind of prayer. Let us seek Him for His workings in our lives so that in our day the Lord, the Judge of all, would find one who would stand in the gap (see the book *Practicing His Presence* for more teaching on this subject).

B. A Few Essentials

A few essential things this type of intercession requires:

1. People willing to look with eyes open and see the condition of the people without justifying their actions.
2. People willing to give up their life.
3. A broken heart.
4. Grace to carry the burdens.
5. Desperate people willing, if necessary, to be used in the answer to their prayers.

II. CONFESSION IN INTERCESSION

A. Sin is a Block that Must be Removed

Remember, we are **not** dealing with the sin or actions of the individual who is praying (that should already be taken care of), but the sin or condition of another or even of an entire nation!

1. Ps. 66:18 – *If I regard iniquity in my heart, the Lord will not hear me.*
2. Prov. 28:9 – *He who turns away his ear from listening to the law, even his prayer is an abomination.*
3. Prov. 15:8 – *The sacrifice of the wicked is an abomination to the Lord, but the prayer of the upright is His delight.*

B. Daniel's Example

1. Meditation on the Word. Daniel was pondering on the words of Jeremiah 29:10-14 (as stated in Dan. 9:2). He apparently was convicted and enlightened by the scripture.
2. He did not respond presumptuously, but rather sought for the Spirit's remedy so the promise could be fulfilled.
3. As he meditated on God's prophetic desire, he realized there were blockades that must be removed before the promise would be fulfilled.
4. He laid aside self-justification (Lk. 18:12-13; the Pharisee and Publican syndrome).
5. Daniel confessed **their** sin as **his** own (Dan. 9:4-17).
6. Then he pleaded with the Lord for mercy for His own Name's sake (Dan. 9:18-19).

C. Nehemiah's Example

1. A report was brought to Nehemiah that saddened his heart. *And they said to me, 'The remnant there in the province who survived the captivity are in great distress and reproach, and the wall of Jerusalem is broken down and its gates are burned with fire* (Neh. 1:3).
2. *He then wept and mourned for days; ...fasting and praying before the God of heaven under this burden* (Neh. 1:4).
3. This resulted in petitions beginning with respect and adoration (Neh. 1:5).

4. He then confessed the sin of the sons of Israel saying, I and my fathers' house have sinned. We have acted very corruptly against Thee (Neh.1:6-7).
5. He then reminded God of His prophetic promise to Moses (Neh.1:8-9).
6. Nehemiah made an appeal to God on the basis of His redemptive work which He has done (Neh.1:10).
7. He then implored God for favor with the King and asked for success (Neh.1:11).

D. Ezra's Example

1. The princes approached Ezra with a report concerning the abominations of the people; the priests and the Levites were intermarrying with the people of the land (Ezra 9:1-2).
2. Ezra then tore his garment and robe, plucked some of his hair and beard, and sat down appalled (Ezra 9:3).
3. Those who *trembled at the words of God* joined Ezra in shock and humiliation (Ezra 9:4).
4. Ezra then arose from his humiliation (fasting), fell on his knees and hands, and began to cry out to the Lord (Ezra 9:5).
5. He names the sin as a priestly spokesman before God as his own and states "their" iniquities, guilt, shame, and embarrassment (Ezra 9:6-7). Notice the complete absence of a self-righteous attitude.
6. He recalls God's grace, faithfulness, and loving kindness, and amid all of the sin, gives them a purpose of revival and restoration (Ezra 9:8-9).
7. He acknowledges that God has requited them less than their iniquities deserve (Ezra 9:10-13).
8. 8. He speaks to the Lord concerning the importance of maintaining the remnant (Ezra 9:14-15).
9. Ezra weeps bitterly with repentance before the house of God (Ezra 10:1).
10. Shecaniah joins in the cry for repentance and says they will put aside their wrong doings and make a covenant with God and follow Ezra in the path of righteousness and restoration (Ezra 10:2-4).
11. Ezra calls the offenders forward over a three-day period to publicly repent (Ezra 10:5-8).
12. They are charged with their sin and personal confession is made with a vow to do what is right (Ezra 10:9-17).

E. From the Life of Praying Hyde

Praying Hyde reports learning an important lesson concerning fault-finding. Seldom in public did critical words of a piercing nature flow from his lips. In his prayer life, however, this was not the case. Once he felt a keen burden on his heart for a native Indian pastor. Upon entering his favorite place of prayer, he developed a bitter spirit toward this pastor's mannerisms. In his mind he criticized that pastor and began praying a bitter prayer: "Oh, Father, Thou knowest how cold..." but something stopped him in the midst of prayer. A finger seemed to touch Hyde's lips, sealing them shut. He heard the voice of God softly say, "He that toucheth him, toucheth the apple of mine eye." Praying Hyde at once cried out, "Forgive me, Father, in that I have been an accuser of the brethren before Thee." In the anguish of prayer, Hyde begged God to show him good things in this pastor's life and as moments passed, good points saturated Hyde's mind. As each good quality came to mind, Hyde stopped and praised God for this dear pastor.

Soon after Hyde's prayer, revival hit the Indian church. Clearly felt was the impact of a loving spirit. Let it never be forgotten – forgiving hearts are parents to revival. The love gives birth to God's outpouring.[20]

F. From the Life of Rees Howell – Bible Teacher and Intercessor

"These three aspects," taught Howell, "are never found in ordinary prayer." Included, first of all, is **identification**: law number one for every intercessor. Christ remains the supreme example of this crucial law. He was numbered with transgressors. He became the High Priest interceding on our behalf. Christ came to earth from ivory palaces, born in a humble manger. God's Son pitched His tent within our camp, making Himself a brother to all men. Temptation became a snare to Him and death the taste upon His lips. He suffered with the suffering and walked the rocky roads we mortals walk. Jesus epitomized lasting love. His lovely life defines the **intercessor: one who identifies with others.**

Howell listed **agony** as the second law of the intercessor. "If we are to be an intercessor," felt Howell, "we must be fully like the Master."

The author of Hebrews 5:7 says our Master prayed with... *strong crying and tears.* The apostle Paul says in Romans 8:26 ...*the Spirit itself maketh intercession for us with groanings which cannot be uttered.*

Jesus reached deepest depths in the sea of agony; Gethsemane, no doubt, was the ocean floor. Here is destined the agony of agonies. Here our Master's heart was broken as none have known. His life teaches **intercession's key: to agonize for souls.**

Howell's third law concerns **authority.** He states, "If the intercessor is to know identification and agony, he also knows authority. He moves God, this intercessor. He even causes Him to change His mind." Howell claimed that when he gained a place of intercession for a need, and believed it God's will, he always had a victory.[21]

G. The Cry of Moses
After the children of Israel had gone astray and made a god of gold for themselves, the deep and desperate plea of Moses was, *But now, if Thou wilt, forgive their sin – and if not, please blot me out from Thy Book which Thou hast written* (Ex. 32:32).

H. Paul the Apostle's Burden
In Romans 9 and 11, it portrays the intercessory cry of Paul, an apostle to the Gentiles, for his kinsmen after the flesh – the Israelites. Romans 9:1-3 tells us, *I am telling you the truth in Christ. I am not lying, my conscience being my witness in the Holy Spirit, that I have great sorrow and unceasing grief in my heart. For I could wish that I myself were accursed, separated from Christ for the sake of my brethren, my kinsmen according to the flesh.*

III. INTERCESSION AND CONFESSION ON BEHALF OF THE WESTERN CHURCHES[22]

A. Following Daniel's Example
Daniel provides a perfect example of the kind of intercession that is needed. He was one of the most righteous men in scripture. His people, Israel, on the other hand, were guilty of persistent rebellion and idolatry. Yet, Daniel didn't pray the prayer of the Pharisee: *God, I thank you that I am not like all other men...* (Lk. 18:11)

On the contrary, in contrition and humility, he identified himself totally with all the failures of his people: *We have sinned and done wrong. We have been wicked and rebelled; we have turned away from your commands and laws* (Dan. 9:5). Daniel's prayer prepared the way for the restoration of Israel from their captivity.

B. Confession – on Behalf of the Western Church

II Chron. 7:14 – *If My people... will humble themselves and pray, ...and turn from their wicked ways...*

1. We have not given Jesus His due headship and preeminence (Eph. 1:22-23; Col. 1:18).
2. We have slighted and grieved the Holy Spirit (II Cor. 3:17).
3. We have not loved one another (Jn. 13:34-35).
4. We have not fulfilled the Great Commission (Mt. 28:18-20; Mk. 16:15-16).
5. We have not cared for the weak and the helpless (Rom. 15:1; Jas. 1:27).
6. We have despised and mistreated the Jewish people (Rom. 11:15-31).
7. We have compromised with, and been defiled by, the spirit of this world (Jas. 4:4; I Jn. 2:15-17).

O Lord, hear! O Lord, forgive! O Lord, listen and take action! (Dan. 9:19).

Reflection Questions
Lesson Five: Identification in Intercession

Answers to these questions can be found in the back of the study guide.

Fill in the Blank

1. _____ is a block that must be removed before interceding.

2. Three aspects not found in ordinary prayer that are found in intercessory prayer are:

   a. _____

   b. _____

   c. _____

3. The _____ Himself maketh intercession for us.

Multiple Choice – Choose the best answer from the list below:

A.	essential	C.	rebellion
B.	iniquity	D.	commission

4. If I regard _____ in my heart, the Lord will not hear me.

5. Many times we are guilty of persistent _____ and idolatry.

True or False

6. One of the essentials of intercession is grace to carry the burdens. _____

7. We should thank God that we are not like the sinner we are praying for because we're better than them. _____

8. Ezra refused to weep for the people before the house of God. _____

Continued on the next page.

Scripture Memorization

9. Write out Psalm 66:18 and memorize it.

10. What was the primary insight you gained from this lesson, and how will you apply it to your life?

Lesson Six:
Christ – Our Priestly Model

I. THE LIFE OF CHRIST

Intercession reached its fullest and most profound expression when our sins were "laid upon" Jesus. It is little wonder that the Bible called it a mystery, hidden deeply within the mind of God! Somehow in the wisdom of God, Jesus was able to fully identify with us, having the totality of our condition placed upon Himself; then as the scapegoat, He carried it far away. There is an aspect of this form of intercession, which we, as His Body, can enter into. It isn't exactly the same as His was, of course, in that His was redemptive in nature. There is, nonetheless, a sharing *on behalf of His body (which is the Church) in filling up that which is lacking in Christ's afflictions* (Col. 1:24).[23]

A. Prophesied by Isaiah

1. Is. 53:12 – *Therefore, I will allot Him a portion with the great, and He will divide the booty with the strong; because He poured out Himself to death, and was numbered with the transgressors; yet He Himself bore the sin of many, and interceded for the transgressors.*

2. Is. 53:6 – *All of us like sheep have gone astray, each of us has turned to his own way; but the Lord has caused the iniquity of us all to fall on Him.*

B. Humbled Himself through Extreme Means
Phil. 2:7-8 – *But emptied Himself, taking the form of a bond-servant, and being made in the likeness of men. And being found in appearance as a man, He humbled Himself by becoming obedient to the point of death, even death on a cross.*

C. Took on the Sins of Mankind

1. II Cor. 5:21 – *He made Him who knew no sin to be sin on our behalf, that we might become the righteousness of God in Him.*
2. Lk. 23:34 – *But Jesus was saying, 'Father forgive them, for they do not know what they are doing.'*

D. Lifts and Carries Away our Transgressions

1. *Nasa* – (From the Hebrew) "To lift up, bear away; remove to a distance."
2. Is. 53:4, 11-12 – *Surely our grief, He Himself bore, and our sorrows He carried; yet we ourselves esteemed Him stricken, smitten of God, and afflicted. As a result of the anguish of His soul, He will see it and be satisfied; by His knowledge the Righteous One, My Servant, will justify the many, as He will bear their iniquities. Therefore, I will allot Him a portion with the great, and He will divide the booty with the strong; because He poured out Himself to death, and was numbered with the transgressors; yet He Himself bore the sin of many, and interceded for the transgressors.*
3. Ps. 103:12 – *As far as the east is from the west, so far has He removed our transgressions from us.*

II. OUR ROLE OF PRIESTLY BURDEN BEARERS[24]

A. Greek Words

1. *Bastazo* – "To lift up, carry" (the idea of carrying off or removing).
   a) Rom. 15:1-3 – *Now we who are strong ought to bear the weaknesses of those without strength and not just please ourselves. Let each of us please his neighbor for his good, to his edification. For even Christ did not please Himself; but it is written, 'The reproaches of those who reproached Thee fell upon Me.'*
   b) Gal. 6:2 – *Bear one another's burdens, and thus fulfill the law of Christ.*

2. *Anechomai* – "Bear up; stake up."
   a) Col. 3:13 – *Bearing with one another, and forgiving each other, whoever has a complaint against anyone; just as the Lord forgave you, so also should you.*
   b) Eph. 4:2 – *With all humility and gentleness, with patience, showing forbearance to one another in love.*
   c) Rom. 12:15 – *Rejoice with those who rejoice, and weep with those who weep.*

B. **The Work of Christ**

1. Mt. 8:17 – *In order that what was spoken through Isaiah the prophet might be fulfilled, saying, 'He Himself took our infirmities, and carried away our diseases.'*
2. Heb. 4:15 – *For we do not have a high priest who cannot sympathize with our weaknesses, but one who has been tempted in all things as we are, yet without sin.*
3. II Cor. 5:18-6:1 – *Now all these things are from God, who reconciled us to Himself through Christ, and gave us the ministry of reconciliation, namely, that God was in Christ reconciling the world to Himself, not counting their trespasses against them, and He has committed to us the word of reconciliation.*

II Cor. 5:18-6:1 continued – *Therefore, we are ambassadors for Christ, as though God were entreating through us; we beg you on behalf of Christ, be reconciled to God. He made Him who knew no sin to be sin on our behalf that we might become the righteousness of God in Him. And working together with Him, we also urge you not to receive the grace of God in vain.*

III. MODELING THE WORK OF CHRIST

A. **Being a Burden Bearer**
We cannot add to what Christ has done, but modeling what He did, we have the burdens and weaknesses of others placed upon us for intercessory purposes. We carry them to the throne, allowing the Holy Spirit to then appropriate the benefits of the Cross, acknowledging and receiving the grace of our Lord and the power of His shed blood as sufficient.

B. **An Invitation into the Life of Identification with Christ**
"Holy Father, grant me Your heart and Your grace for this deepening work of identification in intercession. Open my eyes to see the needs and grant me your broken heart. Help me to lay down my life, grace me to agree with the sin and condition of Your people and help me to carry their burdens. Make me a true intercessor, willing to be an answer to my prayers. Help me, Jesus, to model Your life. For Your Kingdom and Your glory's sake. Amen."

Reflection Questions
Lesson Six: Christ – Our Priestly Model

Answers to these questions can be found in the back of the study guide.

Fill in the Blank

1. All of us like sheep have gone _____.

2. _____ said, "Father forgive them, for they do not know what they are doing".

3. As far as the _____ is from the _____ so far has He removed our transgressions.

Multiple Choice – Choose the best answer from the list below:

    A. intercessor   C. bond-servant

    B. *Anechomai*   D. *Bastazo*

4. _____ means "Bear up; stake up".

5. *Christ taking the form of a* _____ *and being made in the likeness of men...*

True or False

6. We can add to what Christ has done. _____

7. Intercession reached its fullest and most profound expression when our sins were overlooked. _____

8. The Hebrew word *nasa*, means to look away, to ignore. _____

Continued on the next page.

Scripture Memorization

9. Write out II Corinthians 5:21 and memorize it.

10. What was the primary insight you gained from this lesson, and how will you apply it to your life?

# Section Two:

Restoring the "Watch of the Lord"

Lesson Seven:
Fire on the Altar

I. **OVERVIEW OF RESTORATION USING THE OLD TESTAMENT TABERNACLE AS A TYPE**

As we look at the blueprint of the tabernacle of Moses, we see a pattern of restoration of truth and practice throughout church history.

A. THE FIRST STATION:
The Protestant Reformation – 1400 – 1600's

1. Restoration of the altar.
2. Restoration of the sacrifice of the blood.
3. Restoration of justification by faith.

B. THE SECOND STATION:
The Holiness Movement – 1700 – 1800's

1. Restoration of the laver.
2. Restoration of the washing of the hands.
3. Restoration of cleansing and sanctification.

C. THE THIRD STATION:
The Pentecostal Revival – Early 1900's

1. Restoration of the lamp stand.
2. Restoration of the lighting and burning of the seven golden candlesticks.
3. Restoration of the power and gifts of the Spirit.

D. THE FOURTH STATION:
The Charismatic Outpouring – 1960 – 1070's

1. Restoration of the table of shew bread.
2. Restoration of the twelve loaves of bread, representing the twelve tribes of Israel.
3. Restoration of fellowship across the Body of Christ.

E. **THE FIFTH STATION:**
    The Prayer Movement – 1980's and Beyond

    1. Restoration of the altar of incense.
    2. Restoration of the fire continually burning on the altar.
    3. Restoration of worship and prayer.
    4. The time of the incense has come! That the altar of incense has its place nearest to the curtain before the Holy of Holies signifies the spiritual specifics of prayer as coming nearest to the heart of God.

II. OLD TESTAMENT TYPOLOGY

A. The Altar of Incense

1. Ex. 30:1, 7-9 – *Moreover, you shall make an altar as a place for burning incense... And Aaron shall burn fragrant incense on it; ...every morning when he trims the lamps. And... at twilight, he shall burn incense...*
2. Ex. 30:34-38 – *Then the Lord said to Moses, "Take for yourself spices ... and with it you shall make incense...*
3. Lev. 16:2-3, 12 – *...Aaron shall enter the holy place with this: with a bull for a sin offering and a ram for a burnt offering... And he shall take a firepan full of coals of fire from upon the altar before the Lord, and two handfuls of finely ground sweet incense, and bring it inside the veil.*

B. Primary Verses

1. Lev. 6:9-13 – *The fire shall be kept burning continually on the altar. It is not to go out.* These are the verses that inspired Count Zinzendorf and others, including the Moravian prayer meeting, which lasted over one hundred years.
2. Num. 16:46-48 – *And Moses said to Aaron, "Take your censer and put in it fire from the altar, and lay incense on it; then bring it quickly to the congregation and make atonement for them, for wrath has gone forth from the Lord, the plague has begun! Then Aaron took it as Moses had spoken, and ran into the midst of the assembly, for behold, the plague had begun among the people. So he put on the incense and made atonement for the people...*

a) Aaron takes his censor and fills it with fire on the altar. He swings his censor and takes his stand between the dead and the living. The plague is stopped and life comes forth.
b) My wife, Michal Ann was given a dream about the "Cantor" and the Achilles heel. In Greek mythology, a baby was dipped in the water by holding his heel. Every place was protected as he grew up except the backside of his foot (his heel). Michal Ann saw this in a dream and then was told that the medicine for the sore heel was to "go flying with Dr. Cantor." This was a play on words. A "cantor" is a priest who sings his prayers. Our protection is found in swinging our censors filled with the incense of praise and prayers. We are to protect one another rear guard by swinging the censor of prayer.

III. KINGDOM OF PRIESTS

A. New Testament Revelation

1. I Pet. 2:9 – *A royal priesthood... a holy nation.*
2. Rev. 1:6; 5:10 – *A kingdom of priests.*

B. Spiritual Sacrifices

1. Heb. 13:15 – *...praise to God... the fruit of lips that give thanks to His name.*
2. Ps. 100 – *Enter His gates with thanksgiving, and His courts with praise* (v. 4).
3. Rev. 5:1-3, 7-10; 8:3-5. Here we find the golden harp and golden bowl upon the altar in heaven. The incense of prayer fills the bowl, and the harp represents the ministry of praise and worship. The angel takes his censor, fills it with fire on the altar and casts it to the earth.

IV. CURRENT DAY TESTIMONIES

A. Story from Czech Republic – January, 1993
I was standing on the platform before several hundred people in Prague, Czech Republic. The Holy Spirit asked me a question in the middle of my preaching. "Have you ever considered the multi-directional dimension of prayer? Remember, what goes up must come down!"

B. **Testimony from Jackie Pullinger, Missionary in Hong Kong**[25]

Jackie Pullinger told of a Buddhist man named Ali, who had been wrongly imprisoned for a murder. She went to visit him often, but he would not accept Jesus. One day, he was frightened and she told him that she knew a God of justice who knows how he feels. She said she would have people around the world praying and fasting for him on Wednesdays. Later, he did accept Jesus. But how... and why?

He was in his jail cell and the guards smelled a sweet smell. They asked Ali what it was. He did not know. They searched his cell, his possessions, and his person and found nothing. The head of the jail smelled it also. He also searched and found no source for this strange sweet smell.

They left Ali alone and he began to ask questions. "What is this sweet smell they say is here?" Then a thought of revelation came to him. "Oh, it is Wednesday!" He realized they were smelling the incense of prayer and this caused him to accept Christ.

Who smells the sweetness of your prayers?

V. THE LAW AND QUALITIES OF FIRE

A. The Law of the Fire
Leviticus 9:22-24. This fire was...

1. Started by God.
2. Kept burning by the priest.
3. Carried from place to place so that it could be used to start other holy fires. (Same principle applies for renewal and revival – with the Fire of God.)
4. Also see Lev. 10:1-4; 16:12-13; Num. 16:46-50; Gen. 22:6.

B. The Qualities of Fire

1. In the natural, fire:
   a) Purifies
   b) Fuels
   c) Illuminates
   d) Warms
2. In the spiritual, the fire of God:
   a) Sanctifies
   b) Empowers
   c) Enlightens and brings revelation
   d) Warms the heart

VI. THE DIVINE RESPONSE

A. Job 36:32

While I was in Toronto, Canada, I had a dream of scores of lightning bolts coming down. I woke up and saw, in an open vision, Job 36:32 written which states, *He covers His hands with lightning and commands it to strike the mark* (The Hebrew word *paga* means to intercede, or intercession.)

This was nine weeks before the outpouring of the Holy Spirit began there in Toronto, Canada and has spread around the World and is continuing to grow and mature.

B. II Chronicles 7:1-3

*Now when Solomon had finished praying, fire came down from heaven and consumed the burnt offering and the sacrifices; and the **glory of the Lord filled the house**. And the priests could not enter into the house of the Lord, because the glory of the Lord filled the Lord's house. And all the sons of Israel, seeing the **fire come down** and the glory of the Lord upon the house, bowed down on the pavement with their faces to the ground, and they worshipped and gave praise to the Lord saying, "Truly He is good; truly His loving kindness is everlasting."*

Reflection Questions
Lesson Seven: Fire on the Altar

Answers to these questions can be found in the back of the study guide.

Fill in the Blank

1. The _____ shall be kept burning continually on the altar.

2. *Enter His gates with _____ and His courts with _____.*

3. His loving kindness is _____.

Multiple Choice – Choose the best answer from the list below:

      A. The Protestant Reformation   C. The Charismatic Outpouring

      B. The Holiness Movement   D. The Prayer Movement

4. The restoration of the lamp stand came in which movement?
   _____

5. The restoration of worship and prayer came with which movement?
   _____

True or False

6. In Revelation, we find the incense of prayer fills the bowl. _____

7. In the spiritual, fire sanctifies and empowers. _____

8. In II Chronicles 7, *when Solomon finished praying, water came down from heaven and drowned the burnt offering.* _____

Continued on the next page.

Scripture Memorization

9. Write out Psalm 100:4 and memorize it.

10. What was the primary insight you gained from this lesson, and how will you apply it to your life?

Lesson Eight: Restoring the Ancient Tools

I. PROPHETIC WORD

The following is a prophetic word given at Christian Fellowship of Columbia, Missouri by Jane Williams:

The Bride Must Hurry[26]

"There is much I would say to the Church in these days. I would tell you that she is a bride being made ready. I would tell her to busy herself with preparations.

There are invitations to be addressed in the prayer closet. Names to call out from the lists. I will write on your hearts.

There is cake to be made – enough cake to feed all the guests – cake made from the best ingredients: the flour of My Word, the oil of the Holy Spirit, and water from your tears of compassion for the lost and needy. For with these things in combination, you shall make a cake to sustain all who would come.

There are tables to be set. Use white linen tablecloths so that they may know their sins are forgiven. And as you are spreading them over the tables, remember that **your** sins have been forgiven as well, and give Me thanks. Set out glasses for all that I may fill them with the Holy Spirit. The glasses will be your praise and worship, which will bring Me into your presence. The silverware will be your countenances because many will be encouraged to eat of Me because of My glory reflected on your faces. There will be napkins of grace laid everywhere – that each person may give grace to themselves and others – grace to soak up spills and wipe the crumbs from your faces.

And the attendants? Who will your attendants be? I say, the bride's attendants will be mercy and kindness and love for another. These shall be put on display for all to see.

And the words that are to be spoken, what will they be? Come. Come. Come. Come. Again and again it will be repeated. The Spirit and the Bride say, "Come." For an invitation will be extended to all – everyone who is thirsty shall be urged to come. For I would desire that all would come to the wedding feast.

And what about the date? Is it set far in the future that hearts will grow weary in preparation and give up? I say to you, 'No.' The day for the wedding draws near – so near that the Bride must hurry with her work. For an appointed date has been set and the invitations must go out. They must say: 'Come! Come! Come! Eat and drink of the Lord for He has mercy and compassion for all.'

But what about the dress? Who is designing it? Oh, there is no dressmaker fit for the job. It is being designed by God Himself? For He has purchased fine white satin with His very blood and is detailing it to perfection. Beads of His righteousness, pearls of His love, lace made from His mercy and grace. For the bride is to be spectacular, the glory and reflection of God Himself. For she will have no spot or wrinkle but be perfected in every way.

And will the two unite? This bride and groom? Oh, yes, for their hearts are one and they will give themselves freely to each other. There will be no holding back at this moment of the culmination of the age. They will dance. They will gaze upon each other and know the sweet kisses of love and the hearts of all will be made glad."

Here we are given an example of our prayers being used like "invitations" to a wedding waiting to be sent out.

II. ANCIENT TOOLS

A. A Vision of a Plow in the Night
While leading a prayer retreat in June, 1991, our prayer team was doing night and morning watches. While on my "watch" at 2:00 a.m., I saw a vision of an old plow. I asked the Lord, "What is this?" He responded, "These are the ancient tools." The phrase then came to me, "The watch of the Lord is an ancient tool. The watch of the Lord has been used and will be used again to change the expression of Christianity across the face of the earth."

B. Little Keys Open Big Doors!

1. Mt. 18:19-20 – *"Again I say to you, that if two of you agree on earth about anything that they may ask, it shall be done for them by My Father who is in heaven. For where two or three have gathered together in My name, there I am in their midst."*
    a) Two or three.
    b) Led together in His Name.
    c) Harmonizing.

         d) Ask!
         e) Answers come!
         f) God's manifested presence comes!

    2. Lk. 11:52 – *Woe to you lawyers! for you have taken away the key to knowledge; you did not enter in yourselves, and those who were entering in you hindered.*

Let's not be like the "lawyers" who had the keys of knowledge and would misuse them. Let's take the keys of the Kingdom and open heaven's big doors and enter in.

III. SCRIPTURAL RESPONSES TO THE LAST DAYS

A comparative study of the words Jesus said His disciples were to do in the time of the "Last Days" (taken from the NIV).

A. Matthew 24

   1. Watch out that no one deceives you (v. 4).
   2. See to it that you are not alarmed (v. 6).
   3. Stand firm to the end (v. 13).
   4. Keep watch (v. 42).

B. Mark 13

   1. Watch out that no one deceives you (v. 5).
   2. Do not be alarmed (v. 7).
   3. Be on your guard (v. 9).
   4. Do not worry (v. 11).
   5. Stand firm (v. 13).
   6. Be on your guard (v. 23).
   7. Be on your guard; be alert (v. 33).
   8. Keep watch (v. 35).
   9. Watch out (v. 37).

C. Luke 21

   1. Watch out that you are not deceived (v. 8).
   2. Do not be frightened (v. 9).
   3. Stand firm (v. 19).
   4. Stand up and lift up your heads (v. 28).
   5. Be careful (v. 34).
   6. Be always on the watch and pray (v. 36).

D. Comparison of these Three Great Chapters

1. "Do not be afraid" – four times.
2. "Stand firm" – four times.
3. "Watch" – eleven times.

Almost three times more than anything else, Jesus said to "watch".

IV. LESSONS FROM GIDEON

A. Read Judges 6

1. Gideon is visited by the angel of the Lord and called a "valiant warrior" – Judg. 6:1-16.
2. Gideon's charge to destroy the enemy's altar – Judg. 6:25-27.
3. Gideon destroys the altar – Judg. 6:28-30.
4. A penalty placed upon Gideon by his father – Judg. 6:31-32.
5. Gideon's reward for obedience – Judg. 6:33-35.
   a) The Spirit of the Lord came upon Gideon, clothed him with Himself, and took possession of Him!
   b) God wants us to "be possessed!" Get possessed by God!

B. Read Judges 7:2-6

1. Judg. 7:2-3 – *Let all the fearful depart.* 32,000 began and 22,000 returned home. Only 10,000 remained.
2. Judg. 7:4-6 – *Take them to the water to drink.* 9,700 kneeled on both knees to drink water. All they could see was a reflection of themselves. 300 put their hands to their mouth and lapped the water like a dog. This portrayed the power of **watching and guarding** while yet partaking. These 300 were chosen.
3. This illustration of Gideon and his army is similar to the lessons of the three Gospel accounts. We must overcome our fears to be able to stand firm so that we can watch over that which God has given.

V. LESSONS FROM THE MORAVIANS

A Prayer Meeting that Lasted 100 Years [27] by Leslie K. Tarr

FACT: The Moravian community of Herrnhut, Saxony, in 1727, commenced an around-the-clock "prayer watch" that continued non-stop for over a hundred years.

FACT: By 1792, 65 years after commencement of that prayer vigil, the small Moravian community had sent 300 missionaries to the ends of the earth!

Could it be that there is some relationship between those two facts?
Is fervent intercession a basic component in world evangelization?
The answer to both questions is surely an unqualified "yes."

The heroic eighteenth century evangelization thrust of the Moravians has not received the attention it deserves. But even less heralded than their missionary exploits is that one-hundred year prayer meeting that sustained the fires of evangelism!

During its first five years of existence, the Herrnhut settlement showed few signs of spiritual power. By the beginning of 1727, the community of about three hundred people was wracked by dissension and bickering, an unlikely site for revival!

Zinzendorf and others, however, covenanted to pray and labor for revival. On May 12, revival came. Christians were aglow with new life and power, dissension vanished and unbelievers were converted.

Looking back to that day and the four glorious months that followed, Count Zinzendorf later recalled: "The whole place represented truly a visible habitation of God among men." A spirit of prayer was immediately evident in the fellowship and continued throughout that "golden summer of 1727," as the Moravians came to designate that period. On August 27 of that year, twenty-four men and twenty-four women covenanted to spend one hour each day in scheduled prayer. Some others also enlisted in the "hourly intercession."

"For over 100 years, the members of the Moravian church all shared in the 'hourly intercession.' At home and abroad, on land and sea, this prayer watch ascended unceasingly to the Lord," stated historian A. J. Lewis.

The Memorial Days of the Renewed Church of the Brethren, published in 1822, ninety-five years after the decision to initiate the prayer watch, quaintly describes the move in one sentence: "The thought struck some brethren and sisters that it might be well to set apart certain hours for the purpose of prayer, at which seasons all might be reminded of its excellency and be induced by the promises annexed to fervent, persevering prayer to pour out their hearts before the Lord."

The journal further cites Old Testament typology as warrant for the prayer watch: "The sacred fire was never permitted to go out on the altar (Leviticus 6:13); so in a congregation is a temple of the loving God, wherein He has His altar and fire, the intercession of His saints should incessantly rise up to Him."

That prayer watch was instituted by a community of believers whose average age was probably thirty. Zinzendorf himself was twenty-seven.

The prayer vigil by Zinzendorf and the Moravian Community sensitized them to attempt the unheard-of-mission to reach others for Christ. Six months after the beginning of the prayer watch, the count suggested to his fellow Moravians the challenge of a bold evangelism aimed at the West Indies, Greenland, Turkey, and Lapland. Some were skeptical, but Zinzendorf persisted. Twenty-six Moravians stepped forward for world missions wherever the Lord led.

The exploits that followed are surely to be numbered among the high moments of Christian history. Nothing daunted Zinzendorf or his fellow heralds of Jesus Christ – prison, shipwreck, persecution, ridicule, plague, abject poverty, and threats of death. His hymn reflected his conviction:

> ***Ambassador of Christ,***
> ***Know ye the way we go?***
> ***It leads into the jaws of death,***
> ***Is strewn with thorns and woe.***

Church historians look to the eighteenth century and marvel at the Great Awakening in England and America, which swept hundreds of thousands into God's Kingdom. John Wesley figured largely in that mighty movement and much attention has centered on him. Is it not possible that we have overlooked the place, which that round-the-clock prayer watch had in reaching Wesley and, through him and his associates, in altering the course of history?

One wonders what would flow from a commitment on the part of twentieth century Christians to institute a "prayer watch" for world evangelization, specifically to reach those, in Zinzendorf's words, "For whom no one cared."

VI. THE CALL TO THE WATCH

May the Holy Spirit restore in our day the ancient tools of the "Watch of the Lord." May He awaken us to be vigilant and on the alert, in order to cut off the enemy's plans and usher in God's ambassadors. We welcome the Holy Spirit to speak to us about the part we are to play in being watchmen on the wall. Amen.

Reflection Questions
Lesson Eight: Restoring the Ancient Tools

Answers to these questions can be found in the back of the study guide.

Fill in the Blank

1. *Again I say to you, that if _____ of you agree on earth...*

2. *For where _____ or _____ have gathered together in my name, there am I in their midst.*

3. Let's take the keys of the Kingdom and open _____ big doors and enter in.

Multiple Choice – Choose the best answer from the list below:

    A.   ancient   C.   frightened

    B.   deceives   D.   guard

4. *Watch out that no one _____ you.*

5. *Be on your _____, be alert.*

True or False

6. The Moravian community had a hundred year "prayer watch". _____

7. In the vision of a Plow in the Night, the phrase "the Watch of the Lord is an ancient tool" came. _____

8. In the last days we are to keep watch and stand firm. _____

Continued on the next page.

Scripture Memorization

9. Write out Matthew 18:19 and memorize it.

10. What was the primary insight you gained from this lesson, and how will you apply it to your life?

Lesson Nine:
The Watch of the Lord

I. WATCH DEFINED

A. Biblical Mandate

1. The word "watch" occurs 11 times in three Gospel accounts of Mt. 24, Mk.13 and Lk. 21.

2. The phrase Watch and pray is found in Mt. 26:41 and Mk. 14:38. Matt. 26:41 – *Keep watching and praying, that you may not enter into temptation; the spirit is willing, but the flesh is weak.*

3. Col. 4:2 – *Continue in prayer and watch in the same with thanksgiving.*

B. Definitions of Watch

1. Greek word, *gregoreo* – "to be awake or vigilant"

2. Dictionary definitions for "watch":
   a) "Keeping awake in order to guard"
   b) "A close observation"
   c) "To be on the alert"
   d) "To be alert"

3. Watching is to sleeping as fasting is to eating.

II. SCRIPTURES ON WATCHING

A. Military Terminology

1. II Chron. 23:1-11 – *...And he stationed all the people, each man with his weapon in his hand, from the right side of the house to the left side of the house, by the altar and by the house, around the king. Then they brought out the king's son and put the crown on him, and gave him the testimony, and made him king. And Jehoiada and his sons anointed him and said, "Long live the king!"...*

2. Is. 21:6-12 – *For thus the Lord says to me, "Go, station the lookout, let him report what he sees... Let him pay close attention, very close attention." Then the lookout called, "O Lord, I stand continually by day on the watchtower, and I am stationed every night at my guard post...*

3. I Sam. 11:11 – *And it happened the next morning that Saul put the people in three companies; and they came into the midst of the camp at the morning watch, and struck down the Ammonites until the heat of the day. And it came about that those who survived were scattered, so that no two of them were left together.*

B. Specific Watches Stated in Scripture

1. Ex. 14:24 – The morning watch.
2. Ps. 130:5-6 – Watching for the morning.
3. Mt. 4:25; Mk. 6:48 – The fourth watch.
4. Acts 3:1 – The hour of prayer; the ninth hour.
5. Dan. 6:10 – Three times daily was his custom.
6. Ps. 55:17 – Three times daily prayer ascended.

C. The Task of the Watchman

1. Is. 62:6-7 – To remind the Lord day and night.
2. Lk. 18:1, 7 – To avenge His elect.
3. Hab. 2:1 – To watch and see what the Lord would speak.
4. Prov. 8:34-35 – To listen, wait, and watch daily.
5. I Pet. 4:7 – To be of sober spirit; serious.
6. I Pet. 5:8 – Vigilant (*gregoreo*) to be on the alert.
7. Rev. 3:2 – To bring from death to life.

III. WATCHING IN THE SPIRIT

A. Steps for Watching
To be alert causes us to be aware and have a close observation. We need to be:

1. Spiritually aware of specific world needs.
2. Reflect mentally about "news" of the day.
3. Ask the Holy Spirit to reveal the Father's heart to us.

B. Seeing Things Invisible

1. To "watch" in prayer is to perceive with our spiritual eyes.
2. Jonathan Swift – "Vision is the art of seeing things invisible."[28]
3. Anne Townsend – "If I can imagine what it must be like to be the one for whom I am praying, then I find that I can begin to intercede for that person. My imagination leads me on to want to be more deeply involved with him in his own life. This involvement leads to caring, caring leads to love, and love leads to intercession."[29]
4. I Cor. 2:9-10 – ... *For to us God revealed them through the Spirit; for the Spirit searches all things, even the depths of God.*

IV. PROMISES FOR WATCHMAN

A. Three Great Promises

1. Mt. 26:40-41 – *This is the way of escape from temptation. And He came to the disciples and found them sleeping, and said to Peter, "So, you men could not keep watch with Me for one hour? Keep watching and praying, that you may not enter into temptation; the spirit is willing, but the flesh is weak."*
2. Rev. 16:15 – *Keep your garments clean. "Behold, I am coming like a thief. Blessed is the one who stays awake and keeps his garments, lest he walk about naked and men see his shame."*
3. Mt. 24:42-44 – *This is a way of being prepared. Therefore be on the alert, for you do not know which day your Lord is coming. But be sure of this, that if the head of the house had known at what time of the night the thief was coming, he would have been on the alert and would not have allowed his house to be broken into. For this reason you be ready too; for the Son of Man is coming at an hour when you do not think He will.*

B. Our Goal:
Revelation 20:1-3 ... *And I saw an angel coming down from heaven, having the key of the abyss and a great chain in his hand. And he laid hold of the dragon, the serpent of old, who is the devil and Satan, and bound him for a thousand years, and threw him into the abyss, and shut it and sealed it over him, so that he should not deceive the nations any longer, until the thousand years were completed; after these things he must be released for a short time.*

What is the chain that is used to bind up the devil? Could it be the prayer chain laced with praise?

Reflection Questions
Lesson Nine: The Watch of the Lord

Answers to these questions can be found in the back of the study guide.

Fill in the Blank

1. The Greek word, _____ means to "to be awake or vigilant".

2. _____ and _____ is found in Matthew 26:41 and Mark 14:38.

3. Exodus 14:24 talks about the _____ watch.

Multiple Choice – Choose the best answer from the list below:

      A.   I Cor. 2:9-10   C.   Colossians 4:2

      B.   watchman   D.   sleeping

4. *Continue in prayer and watch in the same with thanksgiving,* is found in _____.

5. Watching is to _____ as fasting is to eating.

True or False

6. Daniel's custom was to kneel before God five times a day in prayer. _____

7. In I Samuel 11:11, no one was left alive after the battle. _____

8. The task of a watchman is simply to watch for danger. _____

Continued on the next page.

Scripture Memorization

9. Write out I Peter 5:8 and memorize it.

10. What was the primary insight you gained from this lesson, and how will you apply it to your life?

Lesson Ten: Possessed for Prayer

Being a House of Prayer

I. **CLEANSING AND PROCLAIMING** [30]

   A. **Jesus Christ Cleansed the Temple**
   Scripture documents that Jesus Christ cleansed the temple of merchandisers who had desecrated and defiled it as a house of prayer.

   1. Mk. 11:17 – *Then He taught, saying to them, "Is it not written, 'My house shall be called a house of prayer for all nations'? But you have made it a den of thieves."*

   2. This event is carefully recorded in each gospel.
      a) Mt. 21:12-13; Mk. 11:15-17; Lk. 19:45; Jn. 2:14-17.
      b) This apparently marks the greatest demonstration of righteous indignation by our Lord.
      c) John's account records that Jesus personally fashioned a whip of cords and then "drove" the transgressors out.
      d) Christ likened the defilement to "a den of thieves," indicating a "den" mentality and "possessive" posture.

   B. **Christ Quotes the Prophet Isaiah**
   Christ quotes the prophet Isaiah and declares that the will, purpose and heart of His Father were violated.

   1. Is. 56:7b – *My house shall be called a house of prayer for all nations.*

   2. God's jealousy is for all peoples.
      a) The "temple of the Lord" is to be marked by prayer for all peoples. (Mk. 11:17, "nations" = "ethnos")
      b) "Prayer for all nations" clearly shows the intended worldwide redemptive intercessory posture, first for Israel and ultimately for the Church of Jesus Christ.
      c) This truth is further exposited in Mt. 28:18-20; Lk. 24:47; Acts 1:8; I Tim. 2:1-8; Rev. 5:9.

II. OUR CALL

A. Worship Is Wholeheartedly Giving Ourselves to God
Worship is the act and Attitude of wholeheartedly giving ourselves to God – Spirit, Soul, and Body.

Pros kuneo (Greek) means "to kiss, like a dog licking his master's hand; to prostrate oneself in homage; to do reverence; to adore."

B. Definition from Webster's Dictionary

1. Intercession is making a request to a superior.
2. Prayer is a means of asking God night and day (Lk. 11:13; 18:8) to release His blessing to touch others; for salvation, healing, anointing or other personal needs. Prayer can be for an individual or for a corporate group of people – a city, church, nation, family group, tribe...

C. Worship and Intercession Go Together!
Revelation 5:8 – *And when He had taken the book, the four living creatures and the twenty-four elders fell down before the Lamb, having each one a harp and golden bowls full of the incense which are the prayers of the saints.*

1. God is seeking both: intercession – Ezek. 22:30; I Tim. 2:1, 8; and worship – Jn. 4:23; II Chron. 7:14.

2. Throughout the Scriptures, expressions of prayer and worship continually appear together.
   a) In the New Testament, those who made requests of Jesus often came worshipping Him – Mt. 8:2; 9:18; 15:25.
   b) Both prayer and expressions of worship are mentioned as integral elements in the early church – Phil. 4:6; Acts 16:25; 13:1-3.

3. In the Old Testament, prayer and praise are not separated. The same Hebrew, as he sang his praise, would pray in slip-stream with his praise. He would never separate the two.
   a) They were uniquely intertwined and never intended to be separated.
   b) Is. 56:7a – *I will ... make them joyful in My house of prayer...* (*tephillah* – a sung intercessory judgment against the enemy).
      (1) The word (*tephillah*) occurs 77 times in the Old Testament and is the most general word for prayer.
      (2) Is used as a title in five Psalms – 17, 86, 90, 102, 142.

- (3) Is the title for the prayer of Habakkuk 3:1.
- (4) Appears in Ps. 72:20 to describe all of Psalms 1-72.
- (5) Denotes a prayer that is set to music and sung in formal worship.
- (6) Hannah's prayer in I Sam. 2:1 – *"My heart exults in the Lord; My horn is exalted in the Lord, my mouth speaks boldly against my enemies, because I rejoice in Thy salvation."*

4. Prayer of Jesus: Mt. 21:13 – *"My house shall be called a house of prayer."* *Proseuo* – Greek word; prose – English: unrhymed poetry, creative and flowing.

III. STORIES FROM HERRNHUT PRAYER ENCOUNTER

A. February, 1993

I led a team of intercessors to recover the anointing of the Moravian prayer watch in Herrnhut, Germany

1. Went with a word that we would meet a man named Christian Winter.
2. We were directed to the number 37. We found Revelation 3:7, which talks about the "key of David."

B. First Stop: Prague, Czech Republic

1. The revelation came while preaching in Prague – "Have you ever considered the multi-directional dimension of prayer? Remember, what goes up, must come down."
2. Our prayer team went to Bethel Chapel. This is the site where Jan Hus preached to the poor seven times on Sundays.

C. The Herrnhut Experience

1. When we first arrived in Herrnhut, a modern-day person named Christian Winter, a spirit-filled, evangelical Moravian, gave me the key to unlock the door of the "watch tower".

2. Stayed in prayer with our group for the first several hours.

3. Then we were "released" to go to the prayer tower.

4. Next we stopped in the cemetery and I sat on Christian David's grave marker. He was the founder of this community of believers.

5. Ezekiel 37 came alive to us. "Can these bones live?" We entered into identification in intercession.

6. We then went to the prayer tower and unlocked the door with the key that the man Christian Winter had given us.

7. Two waves of intercession and a strong wind came upon us as we travailed in Spirit.
   a) The first wave was for calling forth the life or anointing of the past. This was an intercessory act.
   b) The second wave was for sending this anointing for the "watch of the Lord" and a new Pentecost to 120 cities. This was a prophetic release.

8. We looked at the key that had been given to us. It had the number 120 printed on it. This was another confirmation that we had been given a key to the house of prayer for all nations being released to 120 cities and then, like Pentecost, to 3,000 more!

IV. NOW IS THE TIME – BE THE HOUSE OF PRAYER

This is our destiny. This is our call. Let us be possessed by God and His purposes. Let us be possessed for prayer!

"Father, we present ourselves to you for the purpose of prayer. Come Holy Spirit and take possession of us. Fill us with the spirit of grace and supplication in Jesus Name."

Reflection Questions
Lesson Ten: Possessed for Prayer

Answers to these questions can be found in the back of the study guide.

Fill in the Blank

1. *My house shall be called a house of* _____ *for all nations.*

2. In Matthew 21:12, *Jesus* _____ _____ *all who were selling their goods.*

3. _____ means "prostrate oneself in homage".

Multiple Choice – Choose the best answer from the list below:

        A.   Intercession   C.   indignation

        B.   Tephillah   D.   praise

4. Worship and _____ go together.

5. _____ denotes a prayer which is set to music and sung in formal worship.

True or False

6. Because Christ is the Son of God He never got indignant with man. _____

7. Worship is physical activity before God with good intentions. _____

8. God is seeking both intercession and worship. _____

Continued on the next page.

Scripture Memorization

9. Write out Philippians 4:6 and memorize it.

10. What was the primary insight you gained from this lesson, and how will you apply it to your life?

Lesson Eleven:
From Prayer to His Presence

I. THE DISTINGUISHING CHARACTERISTIC

A. From Billy Graham

"What is the greatest hindrance to Christianity?" Some say that AIDS, abortion, war, poverty, sin, atheists, or liberal politicians are. Billy Graham said, "No! The greatest hindrance to Christianity today is Christians who do not know how to practice the presence of God."[31]

B. From A. W. Tozer

"If the Holy Spirit was withdrawn from the Church today, 95 percent of what we do would go on and no one would know the difference. If the Holy Spirit had been withdrawn from the New Testament Church, 95 percent of what they did would stop and everybody would know the difference."[32]

C. Exodus 33:15-16

Then he said to Him, "If Thy presence does not go with us, do not lead us up from here. For how then can it be known that I have found favor in Thy sight, I and Thy people? Is it not by Thy going with us, so that we, I and Thy people, may be distinguished from all the other people who are upon the face of the earth?"

II. REVIEW OF FIRE ON THE ALTAR

A. Five Progressive Stations

1. The altar of sacrifice – the blood of Jesus.
2. The laver – cleansing and sanctification.
3. The lamp stand – power and gifts of the Holy Spirit.
4. The table of shewbread – fellowship of the Body.
5. The altar of incense – ministry of prayer.

B. Moravian History

1. Lev. 6:9-13 – *Fire shall be kept burning continually on the altar; it is not to go out.* (v. 13)
2. In the 1700's, unceasing prayer proceeded forth before the throne for 100 years from the Moravians.

C. Today

1. Czech Republic – In 1993, Jim led a group of intercessors to Czech and to Herrnhut. While ministering in Prague, the Holy Spirit said, "Have you ever considered the multi-directional dimension of prayer? Remember, what goes up must come down."

2. Praying through the 10/40 window on October, 1993, 20 million believers across the face of the earth were united. This was historic. In October of 1995, over 30 million participated in the scheduled campaign "Pray Through the 10/40 Window II". In 1997 the third such event took place with millions of believers praying for the unreached people groups of the earth. Every two years in the month of October this prayer thrust continues, where millions of people worldwide pray for the gospel to go in to those nations.

3. Prophetically, the Church collectively stands at the altar of incense in this hour. This movement continues to grow and progress vastly!

III. THE INCENSE OF PRAYER

A. Primary Scripture

Ex. 30:34-38 – *Then the Lord said to Moses, "Take for yourself spices, **stacte** and **onycha** and **galbanum**, spices with pure **frankincense**; there shall be an equal part of each. And with it you shall make incense, a perfume, the work of a perfumer, salted, pure, and holy. And you shall beat some if it very fine, and put part of it before the testimony in the tent of meeting, where I shall meet with you; it shall be most holy to you. And the incense which you shall make, you shall not make in the same proportions for yourselves; it shall be holy to you for the Lord. Whoever shall make any like it, to use as perfume, shall be cut off from his people."*

B. The Four Qualities of Incense

1. *Stacte* – This means to ooze forth as drops. It is used to describe the "Word of God." We store up the Word and it bubbles forth into prophecy. *Stacte* came from a tree that was a day's journey by walking into Syria. It costs us something to get and store up the Word of God in our lives, also.

2. *Onycha* – This came from the shell of a mussel or mollusk in the Mediterranean Sea. Again, there was a distance to walk to obtain it. It had to be ground into a fine powder and then burned by fire. This gave the incense its sweet odor. Our lives are to be broken before Him (Ps. 51:17). This is the offering that is well-pleasing to Him. Prayer is made up of an equal portion of the Word and brokenness in our lives.

3. *Galbanum* – This means "richness" or "fatness." It is the substance that holds the other ingredients together. We must be "broken," and yet we must *believe that God is a rewarder of those who diligently seek Him.* "He has freely given us all things in Christ Jesus!" This fatness is exhibited through the ministry of grace from the Lord to us. But it is exhibited by a life of faith and praise from us to Him.

4. Frankincense – This fourth element comes from the Hebrew word *lavona*. It means to be white. Prayer has an equal proportion of believing in His gift of righteousness to us. We stand white, pure, and clean before Him. Not because of what we have done or will ever do, but because of what He (Jesus) has already accomplished.

C. The Requirements

1. The ingredients must be gathered from long distances. It costs us something and takes time to develop a true prayer life.
2. It is to be an equal balance of all four ingredients. Some camp around the Word, others emphasize brokenness, still others declare the "fatness" message, while others stress holiness and purity. We are, however, to have a balance of all four.
3. The ingredients had to be made fresh every day. It could not be made ahead of time. We must walk in prayer on a daily basis.
4. Fire has to be added to it. This is our fervency and zeal. Is He worthy of anything less?

D. What Is Prayer?

Prayer is not a methodology. It is more than "Seven Effective Steps." Prayer is more than four qualities equally mixed together. It is communion with God; having a relationship with your Father. Prayer, the power of incense, is life!

IV. THE NEXT STEP

A. From Incense to His Presence

1. *As the priest ministered at the altar of incense, he would take a fire pan filled with fire on the altar and add two handfuls of incense to it (Lev. 16:11-13).*
2. *He would now cross over the threshold into the Most Holy Place. Here rested the Ark of the Covenant with Aaron's rod that budded, a pot of manna from the wilderness wanderings, and the Ten Commandments contained within it. Two covering cherubs faced one another on the lid of the Ark.*
3. *As the priest carried the firepan into the Most Holy Place, a smoke preceded forth and formed a cloud of glory. Between the cherubs was the seat of mercy. This is the place where God would meet with His people (Ex. 25:10-22).*

B. Toronto Word – October, 1994

When in Toronto in October, 1994, the Holy Spirit spoke to me. "I will teach you to release the highest weapon of spiritual warfare." I wondered what would follow. Then He said, "I will teach you to release the brilliance of My Great Presence!"

C. Maintain Your Office – A Dream

I was given a dream where people from Minneapolis, Minnesota were coming to our house to pray with my wife and I. The numbers were growing and we moved to our basement to pray. Then I felt the need to be alone to seek my Master. I had to push away from everyone to get to my office to be alone.

While in my typical prayer posture in my office, my wife was on the other side of the wall re-wiring the house. She was taking out the 110 voltage wires and putting in 220 voltage wiring.

The main interpretation of this dream was that there is a fight to maintain our office before Him. We will bear much fruit as we maintain our office. (Just as New York City is sometimes called the "Big Apple," Minneapolis could be called the "Mini Little Apple." Therefore, Minneapolis symbolized apples, or fruit, in this dream. As we maintain our office and bear fruit, He will rewire our house and perform Galatians 2:20 (the crucified life) in us. The key to it all is maintaining the unique place we each have been granted before Him. By doing this, we will go from prayer to His presence. We will then stand steady in the world and be carriers of the brilliance of His Great Presence.

Reflection Questions
Lesson Eleven: From Prayer to His Presence

Answers to these questions can be found in the back of the study guide.

Fill in the Blank

1. *"If Thy _____ does not go with us, do not lead us up from here."*

2. There are _____ progressive stations at the altar.

3. _____ *shall be kept burning continually on the altar, it is not to go out.*

Multiple Choice – Choose the best answer from the list below:

      A.   prophetically   C.   *Galbanum*

      B.   10/40 Window   D.   communion

4. Prayer is _____ with God.

5. _____ means "richness" or "fatness".

True or False

6. God has freely given us all things in Christ Jesus. _____

7. In 1993, 20 million believers gathered to pray through the 10/40 window. _____

8. The greatest hindrance to Christianity today is politicians. _____

Continued on the next page.

Scripture Memorization

9. Write out Leviticus 6:13 and memorize it.

10. What was the primary insight you gained from this lesson, and how will you apply it to your life?

Lesson Twelve:
The House of Prayer for All Nations

I. CURRENT STATE OF AFFAIRS

A. Statistical Studies

1. There are 33 races of humanity on earth.
2. There are 7,000 language groups among humans on earth today.
3. Every 60 minutes, 7,000 people die. Of these, 6,000 die without Christ.
4. Every 60 seconds 116 die. Of these, 100 go into eternity without Jesus.

B. The Nations

1. There are 235 geographic entities we call nations. By nation, I refer to all geographic entities (ethnic groups – Greek: ethnos) that might be considered distinct countries. Some may be protectorates of larger nations, as Guam is to the United States.[33]
2. Of these, there are 97 nations closed to conventional, residential missionary activity.
3. Today, there are approximately 3 billion people who do not know Jesus.
4. Within the 10/40 Window alone, there are 2.6 billion who do not know Christ.

II. THE REDEMPTIVE FACTOR

A. Psalms 67:1-2

1. *God be gracious to us and bless us, and cause His face to shine upon us – that Thy way may be known on the earth, Thy salvation among all nations.*
2. The Living Bible states, *Send us around the world with the news of your saving power and your eternal plan for mankind.*
3. There is a place where God's face will shine on us. It is the place of prayer! "May the Lord bless you and keep you.
May His face shine on you!"

B. Revelations 5:8-10

1. *And when He had taken the book, the four living creatures and the twenty-four elders fell down before the Lamb, having each one a harp, and golden bowls full of incense, which are the prayers of the saints. And they sang a new song, saying, "Worthy art Thou to take the book, and to break its seals; for Thou wast slain, and didst purchase for God with Thy blood men from every tribe and tongue and people and nation. And Thou hast made them to be a kingdom and priests to our God; and they will reign upon the earth."*

2. Compare Rev. 7:9 – *After these things I looked, and behold, a great multitude, which no one could count, from every nation and all tribes and peoples and tongues, standing before the throne and before the Lamb, clothed in white robes, and palm branches were in their hands...*

3. Compare Rev. 14:6 – *And I saw another angel flying in mid heaven, having an eternal gospel to preach to those who live on the earth, and to every nation and tribe and tongue and people...*

4. While I was ministering in Curaso, Netherlands Antilles. We prayed, worshipped and sang in four languages in the one congregation – English, Spanish, Dutch, and Palpametto. The Holy Spirit said to me, "Do you like this? Wait until you get up here (heaven) – you will really like this."

C. Defining Terms

1. Every tribe – This comes from the Greek word *phulee*, which is translated "tribe", such as the tribe (clan) of Reuben or the tribe of Judah. Because a tribe is not a complete nation, we may conclude that it refers to a smaller group within a nation, such as a cultural group.[34]

2. Every tongue – From the Greek word *glossa*, we get the word "tongue." This refers to languages and dialects – some say one's naturally-acquired language. In the 1980's Wycliffe's Bible Translators passed the 1,000 mark in the number of languages now possessing at least some portion of scripture. However, there are more than 6,000 dialects still waiting![35]

3. Every people – From the Greek word *laos* comes our third focus for the nations. This is used 143 times in the New Testament. It is a reference to people of a particular race without reference to a particular geographic entity.[36] There is said to be three major races from which all three races came forth. These are the Caucasoid (white), Negroid (black), and the Mongoloid (yellow and red).
4. Every nation – The word "nation" comes from the Greek word *ethnos*. It appears 164 times in the New Testament and is commonly translated "Gentiles." (The term refers generally to all nations of the world other than Israel).[37]

III. THE INTERCESSORY FACTOR

A. Who Did Jesus Prophesy Us to Be?

Jesus came and cleansed the temple in Jerusalem and declared that we are to be called ***the house of prayer for all nations!***

1. The liturgical church has primarily made His house into a house of sacraments.
2. The evangelical church has primarily made His house into a house of preaching.
3. The charismatic church has primarily made His house into a house of gifts.
4. But Jesus declared that His house shall be called a house of prayer for all nations.

B. Psalms 2:8

Ask of Me, and I will surely give the nations as thine inheritance, and the very ends of the earth as thy possession...

1. Haitian story – I recall the time I was in Haiti, the poorest country in the Western Hemisphere, teaching on intercession and spiritual warfare. I quoted Psalm 2:8. The pastors began to laugh and say, "You can have this nation." Too often we are too willing to give away what God wants us to keep!
2. Let's ask God for the nations!

C. The Priestly Breastplate

1. The High Priest in the Old Testament wore a breastplate over his heart with 12 stones representing the twelve tribes of Israel.

2. If we are New Testament priests, what stones do you carry on your heart when you come before God? Who are you carrying before God? Do you have a breastplate over your heart?

D. Practical Example from Revelations

1. What is your tribe? Mine is the Goll's, Burns', Willard's, and McCoy's.
2. What is your tongue? Mine is English.
3. What is your ancestry? Mine is German.
4. What is your nation? Mine, of course, is the United States and Israel!

IV. YOUR PRAYERS CAN BRING A WORLD HARVEST!

A. There is Waste in Our Efforts

1. Only a small part is involved in seed sowing.
2. Only a small part of the seed that is sowed germinates.
3. Only a small part of the seed that is sowed and germinates continues to grow and come to full harvest.
4. Only a small part of the actual harvest is actually utilized!

B. Your Prayers Make a Difference!

1. Through prayer you can join any team! Whose team are you on? Join David Wilkerson, Mahesh Chavda, or James Goll's team! Time and distance make no difference. Whose team are you on?
2. You can water the harvest through your prayers. Your prayers release the water upon the seed to bring it forth into productivity!
3. You can cultivate the crop through your prayers. Mt. 13:20-22 says that persecution, anxiety and worries will come. Lift up the prayers of protection and strengthening and watch your planting grow!
4. You can influence world leaders through your prayers. Prov. 21:1 – The king's heart is like channels of water in the hand of the Lord; He turns it wherever He wishes. Change the hearts of rulers through prayer! Be a hidden counselor to those in authority.

C. Contemporary Examples

1. I was on a train for six hours in Germany in the nighttime. The Holy Spirit asked me, "Where are My Daniel's, Esther's, Debra's, and Joseph's?" This came to me over and over!
2. Dick Simmons – Leader of Men for Nations, cried out to the Lord on the bank of the Hudson River, "I beseech Thee Lord, that You send forth laborers into the harvest field!" He was reported at 2:00 a.m. for disturbing the peace as he was praying so loudly. But that night the Holy Spirit fell on David Wilkerson in Pennsylvania and called him to preach in New York City. This began the call to Teen Challenge and a worldwide ministry.

V. THE COLOSSIANS TEN-FOLD CLAIM [38]

Colossians 1:9-12 – *For this reason also, since the day we heard of it, we have not ceased to pray for you and to ask that you may be filled with the knowledge of His will in all spiritual wisdom and understanding, so that you may walk in a manner worthy of the Lord, to please Him in all respects, bearing fruit in every good work and increasing in the knowledge of God; strengthened with all power, according to His glorious might, for the attaining of all steadfastness and patience; joyously giving thanks to the Father, who has qualified us to share in the inheritance of the saints in light.*

A. Five Claims of Revelation

1. Revelation of God's will for the worker – divine direction – *filled with the knowledge of God.*
2. Revelation of God's wisdom for the worker – divine perception – *filled with all wisdom.*
3. Revelation of God's understanding for the worker – divine comprehension – *filled with spiritual understanding.*
4. Revelation of God's holiness in the worker – divine perfection – *walk worthy.*
5. Revelation of God's pleasure in that worker – divine gratification – *unto all pleasing.*

B. Five Claims of Blessing

1. Claim an increase of effectiveness; increased productivity – *fruitful in every good work.*
2. Claim an increase of devotional growth; increased spirituality – *in the knowledge of God.*

3. Claim an increase of strength; increased durability – *strengthened with all might according to God's glorious power.*
4. Claim an increase of patience; increased tenacity – *unto all patience and long-suffering.*
5. Claim an increase of joy; increased delight – *with joyfulness.*

C. Closing Thoughts

Will you personally enlist as a volunteer? Will you let God make **you** into a house of prayer? Will you let God put in **you** His heart for the world?

Blessings to each of you who have studied through this guide.
I trust that you have grown and benefited from these twelve lessons. For more on the subject addressed in this study guide *Watchmen on the Walls*, I commend my book *The Lost Art of Intercession*.

May the Lord Jesus join you in your intercession. May we come into agreement with Him. May the fires be burning continually on the Altar and not go out!

Reflection Questions
Lesson Twelve: The House of Prayer for All Nations

Answers to these questions can be found in the back of the study guide.

Fill in the Blank

1. There are _____ races of humanity on the earth.

2. Every 60 seconds _____ die without knowing Christ.

3. Today there are approximately _____ people who do not know Jesus.

Multiple Choice – Choose the best answer from the list below:

    A.   *Ethnos*   C.   eternal

    B.   *Glossa*   D.   *Phulee*

4. The word "tribe" comes from the Greek word _____.

5. From the Greek word _____ we get the word tongue.

True or False

6. The word "nation" in the New Testament is commonly translated "Gentiles." _____

7. In Revelation, God wills that we would *be full of the knowledge of the world so that we can wage better warfare.* _____

8. God's heart is that we would be *filled with spiritual understanding.* _____

Continued on the next page.

Scripture Memorization

9. Write out Psalm 67: 1-2 and memorize it.

10. What was the primary insight you gained from this lesson, and how will you apply it to your life?

Answers to the Reflection Questions

Lesson One: Our High Calling to Intercession
1. intercession
2. prayer
3. nothing
4. A
5. C
6. True   7. True   8. True

Lesson Two: Definitions and Examples of an Intercessor
1. justice
2. hedge
3. pray
4. C
5. B
6. True   7. False   8. True

Lesson Three: Pleading Our Case
1. reason, Lord
2. pleaded
3. pleas
4. A
5. B
6. False   7. True   8. True

Lesson Four: Presenting Our Case
1. know
2. promise
3. Creator
4. B
5. D
6. True   7. True   8. True

Lesson Five: Identification in Intercession
1. Sin
2. Identity, Agony, Authority
3. Spirit
4. B
5. C
6. True   7. False   8. False

Lesson Six: Christ – Our Priestly Model
1. astray
2. Jesus
3. east, west
4. B
5. C
6. False   7. False   8. False

Lesson Seven: Fire on the Altar
1. fire
2. thanksgiving, praise
3. everlasting
4. A
5. D
6. True   7. True   8. False

Lesson Eight: Restoring the Ancient Tools
1. two
2. two, three
3. Heaven's
4. B
5. D
6. True   7. True   8. True

Lesson Nine: The Watch of the Lord
1. *Gregero*
2. watch, pray
3. morning
4. C
5. D
6. False   7. False   8. False

Lesson Ten: Possessed for Prayer
1. prayer
2. cast out
3. *Pros kunco*
4. A
5. B
6. False   7. False   8. True

Lesson Eleven: From Prayer to His Presence
1. presence
2. five
3. Fire
4. D
5. C
6. True   7. True   8. False

Lesson Twelve: The House of Prayer for All Nations
1. thirty-three
2. one hundred
3. three billion
4. D
5. B
6. True   7. False   8. True

Resource Materials

Elizabeth Alves, *The Mighty Warrior*. Bulverde: Intercessors International, 1987.

Gary Bergel, USA Pray! Training Manual, Reston: Intercessors for America, 1989.

Mike Bickle, *A Personal Prayer List*. Kansas City: Metro Vineyard Fellowship, 1988.

Mike Bickle, *Oasis: Dynamic Intercession*. Milton Keynes: Frontier, 1993.

Paul Billheimer, *Destined for the Throne*, Ft. Washington: Christian Lit Crusade, 1975.

David Blomgren, *Prophetic Gatherings in the Church: The Laying on of Hands and Prophecy*, Portland: Bible Temple Publications, 1979.

Bounds, E. M. *The Complete Works of E. M. Bounds on Prayer*. Grand Rapids: Baker, 1990.

Copeland, Germaine. *A Call to Prayer: Intercession in Action*. Tulsa: Harrison, 1991.

Crist, Terry. *Interceding Against the Powers of Darkness*. Tulsa: Terry Crist Ministries, 1990.

Wesley Duewel, *Mighty Prevailing Prayer*, Grand Rapids, MI: Zondervan, 1990.

Wesley L. Duewel, *Touch the World through Prayer*. Grand Rapids: Francis Asbury, 1986.

Dick Eastman, *Change the World School of Prayer*. Studio City: World Lit Crusade, 1976.

Dick Eastman, *Love on its Knees*. Grand Rapids: Chosen, 1989.

Dick Eastman, *No Easy Road*, Grand Rapids, MI: Baker, 1971.

Dick Eastman, *The Hour the Changes the World: A Practical Plan for Personal Prayer*, Grand Rapids, MI: 1978.

P. T. Forsyth, D.D., *The Soul of Prayer*. Salem: Schmul, 1986.

Richard J. Foster, *Prayer: Finding the Heart's True Home*. New York: HarperCollins, 1992.

Francis Frangipane, *The House of the Lord*. Lake Mary: Creation, 1991.

S. D. Gordon, *What Will It Take To Change The World?*, Grand Rapids, MI: Baker, 1979.

Norman Grubb, *Rees Howells Intercessor*. Fort Washington: Christian Lit. Crusade, 1987.

Kenneth E. Hagin, *The Art of Intercession: Handbook on How to Intercede*. Tulsa: Kenneth Hagin Ministries, 1987.

Graham Kendrick and Steve Hawthorne, *Prayer-walking: Praying On Site with Insight*. Lake Mary: Creation, 1993.

Jack Hayford, *Prayer is Invading the Impossible*. Gwent: Bridge Publishing (U.K.), 1985.

Mary Alice Isleib, *Effective Fervent Prayer*. Minneapolis: Mary Alice Isleib Ministries, 1991.

Cindy Jacobs, *Possessing the Gates of the Enemy*. Tarrytown: Fleming H. Revell, 1991.

Dr. Larry Lea, *Could You Not Tarry One Hour?* Rockwell: Creation, 1985.

Gordon Lindsay, *Prayer and Fasting: The Master Key to the Impossible*. Dallas: Christ for the Nations, Inc., 1979.

Martyn Lloyd-Jones, *Enjoying the Presence of God*, Michigan: Vine, 1992.

Andrew Murray, *With Christ in the School of Prayer*, Springdale: Whitaker, 1981.

Derek Prince, *Blessing or Curse: You Can Choose!* Old Tappan: Chosen, 1990.

Derek Prince, *Fasting*. Fort Lauderdale: Derek Prince Ministries, 1986.

Derek Prince, *How to Fast Successfully*. Fort Lauderdale: Derek Prince Ministries, 1976.

Derek Prince, *Praying for the Government*. Fort Lauderdale: Derek Prince Publications, 1970.

Derek Prince, *Shaping History Through Prayer and Fasting*. Fort Lauderdale: Derek Prince Ministries, 1973.

Derek and Ruth Prince, *Prayers and Proclamations*. Fort Lauderdale: Derek Prince Ministries – International, 1990.

Jackie Pullinger, "Metro Christian Fellowship Missions Conference", 1993.

Leonard Ravenhill, *A Treasury of Prayer: The Best of E. M. Bounds on Prayer in a Single Volume*. Minneapolis: Bethany, 1981.

Leonard Ravenhill, *Revival Praying*. Minneapolis: Bethany, 1962.

Leonard Ravenhill, *Why Revival Tarries*. Minneapolis: Bethany, 1959.

Gwen Shaw, *Redeeming the Land*. Jasper: Engeltal, 1987.

Dutch Sheets, *Intercessory Prayer – The Lightning of God*, Dallas: 1986.

Ed Silvoso, *That None Should Perish: How to Reach Entire Cities for Christ Through Prayer Evangelism*. Ventura: Regal, 1994.

A. B. Simpson, *The Life of Prayer*. Camp Hill: Christian Pub, 1989.

Kjell Sjoberg, *Winning the Prayer War*. Chicester: New Wine, 1991.

Mary Ruth Swope, *Listening Prayer*. Springdale: Whitaker, 1987.

Leslie K. Tarr, *Decision Magazine*, May, 1997.

Mark and Patti Virkler, *Communion with God*. Shippensburg: Destiny Image, 1990.

C. Peter Wagner, *Engaging the Enemy: How to Fight and Defeat Territorial Spirits*. Ventura: Regal, 1991.

C. Peter Wagner, *Prayer Shield*. Ventura: Regal, 1995.

C. Peter Wagner, *Warfare Prayer*. Ventura: Regal, 1992.

Arthur Wallis, *God's Chosen Fast*. Fort Washington: Christian Lit Crusade, 1968.

B. J. Willhite, *Why Pray?* Lake Mary: Creation, 1988.

Jane Williams, Prophetic word, Christian Fellowship Church, Columbia, 1996.

John Wimber, *Teach Us to Pray*. Anaheim: Vineyard Ministries International.

End Notes

1. Gary Bergel, *USA Pray! Training Manual*, Reston: Intercessors for America, 1989.
2. Ibid.
3. Ibid.
4. Dick Eastman, *No Easy Road*, Grand Rapids: Baker, 1971.
5. Andrew Murray, *With Christ in the School of Prayer*, Springdale: Whitaker, 1981.
6. Paul Billheimer, *Destined for the Throne*, Ft. Washington: Christian Lit Crusade, 1975.
7. Op. cit., Dick Eastman.
8. Op. cit., Gary Bergel.
9. S. D. Gordon, *What Will It Take To Change the World?* Grand Rapids: Baker, 1979.
10. Dr. Larry Lea, *Could You Not Tarry One Hour?* Rockwell: Creation, 1985.
11. Op. cit., Bergel.
12. Ibid.
13. Dutch Sheets, *Intercessory Prayer – The Lightning of God*, Dallas: 1986.
14. Op. cit., Eastman.
15. Ibid.
16. Op. cit., Murray.
17. Wesley Duewel, *Mighty Prevailing Prayer*, Grand Rapids: Zondervan, 1990.
18. Ibid.
19. Ibid.
20. Op. cit., Eastman.
21. Ibid.
22. Derek Prince, Taken from his teaching ministry, Charlotte.
23. Op. cit., Sheets.
24. Ibid.
25. Jackie Pullinger, Metro Fellowship Christian Ministries Conference, 1993.
26. Jane Williams, Prophetic Word, Christian Fellowship Church, Columbia: 1996.
27. Leslie K. Tarr, Decision Magazine, May, 1997.
28. Dick Eastman, *The Hour That Changes the World: A Practical Plan for Personal Prayer*, Grand Rapids: Baker, 1978.
29. Ibid.
30. Gary Bergel, "The Church: A House of Prayer for All Nations" (handout).
31. Martyn Lloyd-Jones, *Enjoying the Presence of God*, Michigan: Vine, 1992.

[32] Ibid.
[33] Dick Eastman, *Love on Its Knees*, p. 105.
[34] Ibid, p. 107.
[35] Ibid.
[36] Ibid., p. 108.
[37] Ibid., p. 109.
[38] Ibid., pp. 118-121.

About the Author

James W. Goll is a lover of Jesus who co-founded Encounters Network (based in Franklin, Tennessee), which is dedicated to changing lives and impacting nations by releasing God's presence through prophetic, intercessory and compassion ministry. James is the International Director of Prayer Storm, a 24/7/365 prayer media-based ministry. He is also the Founder of the God Encounters Training E-School of the Heart – where faith and life meet.

After pastoring in the Midwest, James was thrust into the role of itinerant teaching and training around the globe. He has traveled extensively to every continent, carrying a passion for Jesus wherever he goes. James desires to see the Body of Christ become the house of prayer for all nations and be empowered by the Holy Spirit to spread the Good News around the world. He is the author of numerous books and training manuals as well as a contributing writer for several periodicals.

He is a member of the Harvest International Ministry Apostolic Team and a consultant to several national and international ministries. James and Michal Ann Goll were married for more than 32 years before her graduation to heaven in the fall of 2008. They have four wonderful adult married children, and James continues to make his home in greater Nashville, Tennessee.

Other Books by James W. and Michal Ann Goll

God Encounters

Prayer Storm

Intercession

A Radical Faith

Women on the Frontlines Series

The Lost Art of Intercession

The Lost Art of Practicing His Presence

The Lost Art of Pure Worship

The Coming Israel Awakening

The Beginner's Guide to Hearing God

The Coming Prophetic Revolution

The Call of the Elijah Revolution

The Prophetic Intercessor

The Seer Expanded

The Seer Devotional and Journal

James W. Goll 365 Day Personal Prayer Guide

Shifting Shadows of Supernatural Experiences

The Lifestyle of a Prophet

Empowered Prayer

Empowered Women

Dream Language

Angelic Encounters

Adventures in the Prophetic

Praying for Israel's Destiny

Living a Supernatural Life

Deliverance from Darkness

Exploring Your Dreams and Visions

God's Supernatural Power in You

The Reformer's Pledge

Prayer Changes Things

In addition there are numerous study guides including Discovering the Seer in You, Exploring the Gift and Nature of Dreams, Prayer Storm, A Radical Faith, Deliverance from Darkness, Prophetic Foundations, Walking in the Supernatural Life, Consecrated Contemplative Prayer and many others with corresponding CD and MP3 albums and DVD messages.

For More Information:

James W. Goll
Encounters Network
P.O. Box 1653
Franklin, TN 37065
Visit: www.encountersnetwork.com
www.prayerstorm.com
www.GETeSchool.com

Email: info@encountersnetwork.com
Speaking Invitations: inviteEN@gmail.com

Resources

Encounters Network
changing lives ❖ impacting nations

P.O. Box 1653 | Franklin, TN 37065-1653
www.encountersnetwork.com | 1.877.200.1604

COMPASSION ACTS
love taking action

Love Taking Action

- **Mission Projects**
  sending resources and volunteers to help meet specific needs
- **Rice Shipments**
  shipping fortified rice to fight hunger around the world
- **Emergency Relief**
  responding to natural disasters through food and humanitarian aid
- **Project Dreamers Park**
  buidling playgrounds and community centers to inspire children to dream
- **First Nations in America**
  serving Native Americans by providing food, health supplies and education

Compassion Acts is a network of synergistic relationships between people, ministries and organizations, focused on bringing hope for our day through the power of compassion and prayer. We desire to demonstrate love and encourage the hearts of those impacted by poverty, disease, political strife and natural disasters through human relief efforts.

www.compassionacts.com

PRAYERSTORM

The Hour that Changes the World

Leviticus 6:13
"Fire must be kept burning on the altar continually; it must not got out."

Worldwide 24/7
Hourly Intercession Targeting:

- **Revival in the Church**
- **Prayer for Israel**
- **World's Greatest Youth Awakening**
- **Crisis Intervention through Intercession**

The vision of **PrayerStorm** is to restore and release the Moravian model of the watch of the Lord into churches, homes and prayer rooms around the world. Web-based teaching, prayer bulletins and resources are utilized to facilitate round-the-clock worship and prayer to win for the Lamb the rewards of His suffering.

Releasing the Global Moravian Lampstand

www.prayerstorm.com

Encounters Network
changing lives ❖ impacting nations

Changing Lives ❖ Impacting Nations

- **Empowering Believers**
  through training and resources
- **EN Media**
  relevant messages for our day
- **God Encounters Training**
  e-school of the heart
- **EN Alliance**
  a coalition of leaders

The vision of **Encounters Network** is to unite and mobilize the body of Christ by teaching and imparting the power of intercession and prophetic ministry, while cultivating God's heart for Israel. We accomplish this through networking with leaders in the church and marketplace; equipping believers through conferences and classes, utilizing various forms of relevant media; and creating quality materials to reproduce life in the Spirit.

www.encountersnetwork.com

GOD ENCOUNTERS TRAINING
e-School of the Heart ~ Where Faith and Life Meet

Introduction to God Encounters Training School

If you are seeking to grow in your intimacy with God and mature in your walk of faith, if you desire to cultivate the spirit of revelation and live a life of power in the Spirit, then begin your journey by joining God Encounters Training – eSchool of the Heart.

Biblically-based study materials in both physical and electronic formats, combined with Spirit-led teaching, are now yours to experience on a personal level. These correspondence courses may be taken for credit towards graduation from the God Encounters Training School.

What Others Are Saying:

Goll's extraordinary ability to think through crucial issues and his skill at expressing the solutions in terms that the average believer can understand, comes through loud and clear in his materials.

   ~ **C. Peter Wagner**, noted author, professor, President of Global Harvest Ministries, Chancellor Emeritus of the Wagner Leadership Institute

The Lord has given James Goll insights into Scripture as it relates to the foundation of each believer and vision for the Body of Christ. His curriculum will powerfully strengthen the spiritual life of any person, group, or congregation that will use them.

   ~ **Don Finto**, author, pastor emeritus of Belmont Church in Nashville, TN and director of the Caleb Company

 For Course Information and Registration Visit **www.GETeSchool.com**

GET eSchool Courses & Corresponding Study Guides

CHAMBER OF ACTION
Exploring Principles - Experiencing Power

Deliverance from Darkness
You shall know the truth and the truth shall set you free! Through this accessible and easy-to-use guide, you will learn how to: recognize demonic entities and their strategies, equip yourself to overcome the demonic, keep yourself refreshed during the fight, bring healing through blessing, and much more!

The Healing Anointing
In this thorough study guide, James W. Goll covers a range of topics including: The Healing Ministry of Jesus, How to Move In and Cooperate with the Anointing, Healing the Wounded Spirit, Overcoming Rejection, the Five Stage Healing Model, and much more.

Releasing Spiritual Gifts
In this study guide, James draws from scripture and adds perspective from many diverse streams to bring you clear definitions and exhort you into activation and release. The topics covered are subjects like: How Does the Holy Spirit Move, What Offends the Holy Spirit, and many other lessons from years of experience.

Revival Breakthrough
James W. Goll brings 12 solid teachings on topics like: Prophetic Prayers for Revival, Classic Characteristics of Revival, Fasting Releases God's Presence, Creating an Opening, Gatekeepers of His Presence, and much more. This manual will inspire you to believe for a breakthrough in your life, neighborhood, region, city and nation for Jesus' sake!

War in the Heavenlies
These carefully prepared 12 detailed lessons on spiritual warfare cover topics like: The Fall of Lucifer, Dealing with Territorial Spirits, The Weapons of Our Warfare, High Praises, The Blood Sprinkled Seven Times, and other great messages. This is one of James' most thorough and complete manuals.

CHAMBER OF LIFE
Building our Foundation - Knowing Truths, Growing in Faith

A Radical Faith
Whether you are a veteran spiritual warrior or new believer, this accessible, comprehensive guide lays out the enduring biblical fundamentals that establish the bedrock of belief for every mature Christian. This handbook will help you build an indestructible foundation of radical faith.

Discovering the Nature of God
These lessons focus on the knowledge of God Himself. Lessons include: Laying a Proper Foundation, The Authority of God's Word, The Effects of God's Word, God as Our Father, The Nature of God, The Attributes of God, Jesus the Messiah, and more. Learn the nature of God and thus be transformed into His image.

Walking in the Supernatural Life
James W. Goll weds together a depth of the Word with a flow of the Spirit that will ground and challenge you to live in the fullness for which God has created you. Topics include The God Who Never Changes, Tools for the Tool Belt, Finishing Well, and much more.

To Purchase these Study Guides Individually & Other Related Product Visit: WWW.ENCOUNTERSNETWORK.COM

  For Course Information and Registration Visit
www.GETeSchool.com

GET eSchool Courses & Corresponding Study Guides

Chamber of Intimacy
Blueprints for Prayer - Prelude to Revival

Watchmen on the Walls

This original study guide is a classic in today's global prayer movement and covers many important and foundational lessons on intercession including: Fire on the Altar, Christ Our Priestly Model, The Watch of the Lord, From Prayer to His Presence, Identification in Intercession, and more.

Compassionate Prophetic Intercession

These 12 lessons feature James W. Goll's finest teaching on the fundamentals of prophetic intercession and represent one of the primary messages of his life. Topics include Travail, Tears in the Bottle, Prophetic Intercession, The Power of Proclamation, Praying in the Spirit, and much more.

Prayer Storm

This study guide sounds a worldwide call to consistent, persistent prayer for: revival in the church, the greatest youth awakening ever, Israel – and for all the descendents of Abraham, and God's intervention in times of major crises. Prayer Storm is an invitation into an international virtual house of prayer full of intercessors who commit to pray one hour per week.

Prayers of the New Testament

In this study guide, James goes through each of the scriptural prayers of the early church apostles and brings you a brief historical background sketch along with insights from the Holy Spirit for today. Learn what true apostolic intercession is, how to intercede with revelation, and how to cultivate a heart for your city and nation.

Strategies of Intercession

In these 12 lessons, James W. Goll deals with issues like Confessing Generational Sins, Reminding God of His Word, Praying for Those in Authority, Praying on Site with Insight, and Praying Your Family into God's Family. It is a thorough and precise exposure to the many different strategies and models of prayer.

Consecrated Contemplative Prayer

These 12 lessons have helped hundreds come into a deeper communion with their heavenly Father. James W. Goll brings understanding from the truths of Christian mystics of the past and builds on it with lessons from his own walk with the Lord. Topics include The Ministry of Fasting, Contemplative Prayer, Quieting Our Souls before God, and much more.

To Purchase these Study Guides Individually & Other Related Product Visit: www.encountersnetwork.com

For Course Information and Registration Visit
www.GETeSchool.com

GET eSchool Courses & Corresponding Study Guides

Chamber of Revelation
Equipping in the Prophetic - Enlisting a Prophetic Army

Prophetic Foundations

Does God really speak to us personally today? If I listen, will I understand what He says? For those desiring to hear God, this course will show how anyone can both listen and speak to God. Lessons include: A Biblical History of the Prophetic, Intimacy in the Prophetic, Seven Expressions of the Prophetic, The Prophetic Song of the Lord, Responding to Revelation, and more.

Maturing in the Prophetic

You can grow in the things of the prophetic! These 12 lessons include: The Calling, Training and Commissioning; The Cross: The Prophetic Lifestyle; Pits and Pinnacles of the Prophetic; The Seer and the Prophet; Women in the Prophetic; and more. Character issues and relational dynamics are discussed at length.

Receiving and Discerning Revelation

This study guide will introduce you to the ways of God and the Spirit of Revelation and how to discern what is from the Holy Spirit and what is not. Learn to grow in your capacity to receive revelatory things from the Holy Spirit, and discern the voice and ways of God with nine scriptural tests to judging revelation.

Angelic Encounters Today

James and Michal Ann Goll use Scripture, church history, testimonies, and personal experience to: describe the different categories of angels, explain angels' ministry as God's agents to the world, demonstrate how intercession and angelic ministry are related, and show you how to perceive and engage angels in your own life.

The Seer

What is the difference between a Seer and a Prophet? How do you cultivate the revelatory presence of the Lord? Is there a key that authentically opens the heavens? This guide helps you find and release the special gifts God has given to you, reveals how you can cultivate this realm of the prophetic in your life, and grounds you in the Word of God concerning prophetic gifts, dreams, visions, and open heavens.

Dream Language

This insightful study guide equips you for a greater understanding of the language of dreams, and grounds you in the Word of God concerning dreams and how to interpret them. This key to unlocking your gift of dreams explores: Cultivating a Culture for Revelation, Dream Drainers, Dream Busters, Why God Seems Silent and How to Cultivate the Realm of the Prophetic in your life.

Understanding Supernatural Encounters

This in-depth study guide contains 12 lessons that will give you insight on subjects like: Prophetic Gestures and Actions, Keys to the Supernatural, The Deception of the Anointing, Trances, Levels of Supernatural Visions, Order and Characteristics of Angels, Ministry and Function of Angels, and much more!

To Purchase these Study Guides Individually & Other Related Product Visit: WWW.ENCOUNTERSNETWORK.COM

  **For Course Information and Registration Visit www.GETeSchool.com**

Made in the USA
Middletown, DE
13 April 2017